THE FATHER'S HEART AND PURPOSE FOR THE END TIMES

Embracing Your Role in His Plan

Stuart D. Bents

To order additional copies of this book, write Father's Heart Book, PO Box 602, Jenks, OK 74037, email fathersheart@liongear.com, or order online at: thefathersendtimeplan.com

Also available at Lion Gear, LLC, email orders@liongear.com, or order online at: liongear.com

ISBN: 0-9907992-0-4
ISBN-13: 978-0-9907992-0-7

DEDICATION

I dedicate this book to my late grandmother Esther, who labored in and exhibited the love and joy of the Lord. And to my grandmother Elsie, who carries the love and joy of the Lord with her on the earth to this very day.

CONTENTS

ACKNOWLEDGMENTS

Thank you, precious Father, for loving us the way you love your Son (John 17). Thank you for loving us enough to send your only beloved Son as a sacrifice for us. Thank you, precious Jesus, for loving us the way the Father loves you (John 15) and for sending your Holy Spirit to help, empower and comfort us (John 14 & 15). Thank you, Holy Spirit, for guiding me, for inspiring me and for revealing to me truth from the Scriptures during the course of this effort.

Thank you, Heidi, my precious and beautiful bride, for being such a great inspiration to me and for allowing me the time to study and seek God's wisdom for this book. Britni, Lucas, Taylor, Olivia, Barrett, Cherish and Braeden—thank you for inspiring me with your courage and fearlessness. Thank you also for your sacrifice of time. I pray that this book becomes an encouraging resource to you in the days and years ahead.

I want to thank our parents, grandparents and great grandparents, including pioneers such as Rev. Gerd Bents and Rev. Harriet McMurray. Thank you, Barbara, for being a pillar for our family these last years. I want to thank all of our spiritual family: mentors, leaders, pastors and teachers— those who went before us, paved the way, provided guidance and direction, built strong foundations and prayed (and still pray) for us. I pray that by the grace of God, your inheritance and testimony will be greatly increased through this work.

I want to thank my sister Wendy and my good friend Brent Orr for the many hours of reading and editing. Your efforts were invaluable. I want to thank Pastor Phil Stern, Dexter Sullivan, Adrian Aizpiri and the many others who provided important input during the course of completing this book.

INTRODUCTION | STAYING CLOSE TO THE HEART OF THE FATHER

As followers of Jesus Christ, I believe the most vital thing we can do as we approach the end of the age is to keep our ears on the heartbeat of the Father as we joyfully anticipate the return of the Son. How do we do this? Jesus says it best, *"Watch and pray!"* (see Mark 13:33 & Luke 21:36).

Despite Jesus' clear instructions, many people may say, "We shouldn't worry about it. It will all just pan out." Well, I do believe the Lord will be panning things out. In fact, He'll be panning for gold! So, my question is, how will it pan out for you?

On the other hand, some people may say, "The Lord gave us a brain! We need to figure out the timing and come up with a plan on what to do!" Yes, of course, He did give us a brain. I think it is interesting that our ears and eyes are the closest organs to our brain. I believe this is a sign that we should primarily be listening to His voice and watching what He is doing. We also need to receive from the Lord through our other three senses. Once we receive His revelation through our spiritual senses, we can then demand the obedience of our mind. We can then use our mind to command the other members of our body. In obedience to the Lord, we will tell our feet to travel and our mouth to bring the good news of the gospel, and to use His words to speak the Kingdom into existence! We will also command our arms to carry out His toil on the earth, preparing the way for His return.

We cannot do things the other way around. We cannot expect to have success by just waiting around and doing nothing. And we cannot just do things that we figure out in our mind and then hope for, or ask for, God's stamp of approval. Instead, like Jesus, we must only do what we see the Father doing and only say what the Father is saying. *We desperately need the mind of Christ, especially in this hour.* We need our mind to be in alignment with God's mind. So, we need to first put our spirit firmly under the control of the Holy Spirit and then put our mind under the obedience of our spirit (or heart). In this way, we will put our ears on the heartbeat of God. Like John the Apostle, who called himself *"the disciple whom Jesus loved,"* we will lean our head on the breast of Jesus (see John 13:23). What did John receive by doing this? He received much more than he expected—he received the greatest Revelation!

We also know that timing is very important. We see this in Jesus' words as He wept over Jerusalem.

> *As he approached Jerusalem and saw the city, he wept over it and said, "If you, even you, had only known on this day what would bring you peace—but now it is hidden from your eyes. The days will come upon you when your enemies will build an embankment against you and encircle you and hem you in on every side. They will dash you to the ground, you and the children within your walls. They will not leave one stone on another, because you did not recognize the time of God's coming to you." (Luke 19:41-44)*

However, knowing God's heart and hearing His voice is more important than just knowing timing. For when we hear God's heartbeat and hear His voice, we discover His heart and purpose for the end times. Furthermore, when we begin to hear the Father's heartbeat, we will inherently begin to recognize the subtleties of His timing.

Our precious Bridegroom God is pressing in and searching our hearts in deeper ways, exposing intricate, complex and hidden issues. At the same time, He is exposing a greater revelation of His glorious and passionate heart!

This book contains discussion, stories and commentary, but is primarily composed of scripture. In various chapters throughout the book you will encounter individual scriptures, or even short lists of scriptures, that will encompass a certain theme. As you read through these scriptures, ask the Holy Spirit to reveal the heart of the Father to you concerning the specific theme being addressed. Here are a few scriptures that will help prepare our hearts to get started into the book.

But if from there you seek the Lord your God, you will find him if you seek him with all your heart and with all your soul. (Deuteronomy 4:29)

Call to me and I will answer you and tell you great and unsearchable things you do not know. (Jeremiah 33:3)

...we declare God's wisdom, a mystery that has been hidden and that God destined for our glory before time began. None of the rulers of this age understood it, for if they had, they would not have crucified the Lord of glory. However, as it is written: 'What no eye has seen, what no ear has heard, and what no human mind has conceived'— the things God has prepared for those who love him—these are the things God has revealed to us by his Spirit. The Spirit searches all things, even the deep things of God. For who knows a person's thoughts except their own spirit within them? In the same way no one knows the thoughts of God except the Spirit of God. What we have received is not the spirit of the world, but the Spirit who is from God, so that we may understand what God has freely given us. This is what we speak, not in

words taught us by human wisdom but in words taught by the Spirit, explaining spiritual realities with Spirit-taught words. The person without the Spirit does not accept the things that come from the Spirit of God but considers them foolishness, and cannot understand them because they are discerned only through the Spirit. The person with the Spirit makes judgments about all things, but such a person is not subject to merely human judgments, for, "Who has known the mind of the Lord so as to instruct him?" But we have the mind of Christ. (1 Corinthians 2:7-16)

"Ask and it will be given to you; seek and you will find; knock and the door will be opened to you." (Matthew 7:7)

You will keep in perfect peace those whose minds are steadfast, because they trust in you. (Isaiah 26:3)

My son, pay attention to what I say; turn your ear to my words. Do not let them out of your sight, keep them within your heart; for they are life to those who find them and health to one's whole body. Above all else, guard your heart, for everything you do flows from it. Keep your mouth free of perversity; keep corrupt talk far from your lips. Let your eyes look straight ahead; fix your gaze directly before you. Give careful thought to the paths for your feet and be steadfast in all your ways. Do not turn to the right or the left; keep your foot from evil. (Proverbs 4:20-27)

But solid food is for the mature, who because of practice have their senses trained to discern good and evil. (Hebrews 5:14, NASB)

Taste and see that the Lord is good; blessed is the one who takes refuge in him. (Psalm 34:8)

The path of the righteous is like the morning sun, shining ever brighter till the full light of day. But the way of the wicked is like deep darkness; they do not know what makes them stumble. (Proverbs 4:18-19)

O people of Zion, who live in Jerusalem, you will weep no more. How gracious he will be when you cry for help! As soon as he hears, he will answer you. Although the Lord gives you the bread of adversity and the water of affliction, your teachers will be hidden no more; with your own eyes you will see them. Whether you turn to the right or to the left, your ears will hear a voice behind you saying, "This is the way; walk in it."' Then you will defile your idols overlaid with silver and your images covered with gold; you will throw them away like a menstrual cloth and say to them, "Away with you!" (Isaiah 30:19-22)

1 | THE OIL OF JOY—THE BRIDEGROOM COMETH!

There is Going to Be a Wedding

The Father's heart and purpose for the end of the age can be found throughout His Book. The Father had promised His Son, Jesus Christ, that He would provide for Him an inheritance, a people all His own, prepared from the foundations of the earth. The Father and the Son both passionately love us—His inheritance, His Church, His Bride! The Lamb of God, Jesus Christ, paid the price for us; His body was broken and His blood was shed for our healing and the remission of our sins. He will be married to us, His people, forever! He will walk with us in the cool of the day. He will rule and reign with us on the earth. It is the restoration of all things. It is the new beginning! This new beginning will burst forth into existence on the earth, revealing the way that God intended it to be from the very beginning!

A New Heaven and a New Earth

Then I saw "a new heaven and a new earth," for the first heaven and the first earth had passed away, and there was no longer any sea. I saw the Holy City, the new Jerusalem, coming down out of heaven from God, prepared as a bride beautifully dressed for her husband. And I heard a loud voice from the throne saying, "Look! God's dwelling place is now among the people, and he will dwell with them. They will be his people, and God himself will be with them and be their God. 'He will wipe every tear from their eyes. There will be no more death' or mourning or crying or pain, for the old order of things has passed away."

He who was seated on the throne said, "I am making everything new!" Then he said, "Write this down, for these words are trustworthy and true."

He said to me: "It is done. I am the Alpha and the Omega, the Beginning and the End. To the thirsty I will give water without cost from the spring of the water of life. Those who are victorious will inherit all this, and I will be their God and they will be my children. But the cowardly, the unbelieving, the vile, the murderers, the sexually immoral, those who practice magic arts, the idolaters and all liars—they will be consigned to the fiery lake of burning sulfur. This is the second death."

The New Jerusalem, the Bride of the Lamb

One of the seven angels who had the seven bowls full of the seven last plagues came and said to me, "Come, I will show you the bride, the wife of the Lamb." And he carried me away in the Spirit to a mountain great and high, and showed me the Holy City, Jerusalem, coming down out of heaven from God. It shone with the glory of God, and its brilliance was like that of a very precious jewel, like a jasper, clear as crystal. It had a great, high wall with twelve gates, and with twelve angels at the gates. On the gates were written the names of the twelve tribes of Israel. There were three gates on the east, three on the north, three on the south and three on the west. The wall of the city had twelve foundations, and on them were the names of the twelve apostles of the Lamb.

The angel who talked with me had a measuring rod of gold to measure the city, its gates and its walls. The city was laid out like a square, as long as it was wide. He measured the city with the rod and found it to be 12,000 stadia in length, and as wide and high as it is long. The angel measured the wall using human measurement, and it was 144 cubits thick. The wall was made of jasper, and the city of pure gold, as pure as glass. The foundations of the city walls were decorated with every kind of precious stone. The first foundation was jasper, the second sapphire, the third agate, the fourth emerald, the fifth onyx, the sixth ruby, the seventh chrysolite, the eighth beryl, the ninth topaz, the tenth turquoise, the eleventh jacinth, and the twelfth amethyst. The twelve gates were twelve pearls, each gate made of a single pearl. The great street of the city was of gold, as pure as transparent glass.

I did not see a temple in the city, because the Lord God Almighty and the Lamb are its temple. The city does not need the sun or the moon to shine on it, for the glory of God gives it light, and the Lamb is its lamp. The nations will walk by its light, and the kings of the earth will bring their splendor into it. On no day will its gates ever be shut, for there will be no night there. The glory and *honor of the nations will be brought into it. Nothing impure will ever enter it, nor will anyone who does what is shameful or deceitful, but only those whose names are written in the Lamb's book of life.*

Eden Restored

Then the angel showed me the river of the water of life, as clear as crystal, flowing from the throne of God and of the Lamb down the middle of the great street of the city. On each side of the river stood the tree of life, bearing twelve crops of fruit, yielding its fruit every month. And the leaves of the tree are for the healing of the nations. No longer will there be any curse. The throne of God and of the Lamb will be in the city, and his servants will serve him. They will see his face, and his name will be on their foreheads. There will be no more night. They will not need the light of a lamp or the light of the sun, for the Lord God will give them light. And they will reign for ever and ever.

John and the Angel

The angel said to me, "These words are trustworthy and true. The Lord, the God who inspires the prophets, sent his angel to show his servants the things that must soon take place."

"Look, I am coming soon! Blessed is the one who keeps the words of the prophecy written in this scroll." (Revelation 21:1-22:7)

We must understand that Jesus is very passionate about His Bride! The Scriptures are very clear about this, yet we often struggle to comprehend it.

Our Bridegroom says to us,

"Place me like a seal over your heart, like a seal on your arm; for love is as strong as death, its jealousy unyielding as the grave. It burns like blazing fire, like a mighty flame. Many waters cannot quench love; rivers cannot sweep it away. If one were to give all the wealth of one's house for love, it would be utterly scorned." (Song of Songs 8:6-7)

We, the Bride, respond to the Bridegroom,

"I am a rose of Sharon, a lily of the valleys." (Song of Songs 2:1)

The Bridegroom responds to the Bride,

"Like a lily among thorns is my darling among the young women." (Song of Songs 2:2)

Our Bridegroom not only adores the Bride, He is also very concerned about her current state of self-imposed suffering. His desire is to gather her to Himself and to be her protection and covering.

"Jerusalem, Jerusalem, you who kill the prophets and stone those sent to you, how often I have longed to gather your children together, as a hen gathers her chicks under her wings, and you were not willing. Look, your house is left to you desolate." (Matthew 23:27-28)

"To me this is like the days of Noah, when I swore that the waters of Noah would never again cover the earth. So now I have sworn not to be angry with you, never to

rebuke you again. Though the mountains be shaken and the hills be removed, yet my unfailing love for you will not be shaken nor my covenant of peace be removed," says the Lord, who has compassion on you. "Afflicted city, lashed by storms and not comforted, I will rebuild you with stones of turquoise, your foundations with lapis lazuli. I will make your battlements of rubies, your gates of sparkling jewels, and all your walls of precious stones. All your children will be taught by the Lord, and great will be their peace. In righteousness you will be established: Tyranny will be far from you; you will have nothing to fear. Terror will be far removed; it will not come near you. If anyone does attack you, it will not be my doing; whoever attacks you will surrender to you. See, it is I who created the blacksmith who fans the coals into flame and forges a weapon fit for its work. And it is I who have created the destroyer to wreak havoc; no weapon forged against you will prevail, and you will refute every tongue that accuses you. This is the heritage of the servants of the Lord, and this is their vindication from me,' declares the Lord." (Isaiah 54:9-17)

Due to the immeasurable largeness of His heart, our Bridegroom is bursting with love for us! His intention is to abide with us forever. Therefore, our Savior and King is firm and resolute about His wedding plans. It will happen as He has promised! Throughout history, and ever increasingly, He has had intercessors praying His wedding plans into reality. Will you join with them?

No longer will they call you Deserted, or name your land Desolate. But you will be called Hephzibah, and your land Beulah; for the Lord will take delight in you, and your land will be married. As a young man marries a young woman, so will your Builder marry you; as a bridegroom rejoices over his bride, so will your God rejoice over you. I have posted watchmen on your walls, Jerusalem; they will never be silent day or night. You who call on the Lord, give yourselves no rest, and give him no rest till he establishes Jerusalem and makes her the praise of the earth. (Isaiah 62:4-7)

As we look forward into the future, we see the beauty, splendor, glory and nobility of the Bridegroom as He returns for His wedding day. The scene can be found in the book of Psalms, chapter 45. This is His triumphant return! It is the day that the Bridegroom will be married to the Bride. In the Psalms, it is appropriately named, *"A Wedding Song"* and even sung, *"To the tune of 'Lilies'"* (see Song of Songs 2:1-2 above).

My heart is stirred by a noble theme as I recite my verses for the king; my tongue is the pen of a skillful writer. You are the most excellent of men and your lips have been anointed with grace, since God has blessed you forever. Gird your sword on your side, you mighty one; clothe yourself with splendor and majesty. In your majesty ride forth victoriously in the cause of truth, humility and justice; let your right hand achieve awesome deeds. Let your sharp arrows pierce the hearts of the king's enemies; let the nations fall beneath your feet. Your throne, O God, will last for ever and ever; a scepter of justice will be the scepter of your kingdom. You love righteousness and hate wickedness; therefore God, your God, has set you above your companions by anointing you with the oil of joy. All your robes are fragrant with myrrh and aloes and cassia; from palaces adorned with ivory the music of the strings makes you glad. Daughters of kings are among your honored women; at your right hand is the royal bride in gold of Ophir [See Isaiah 13:12]. Listen, daughter, and pay careful attention: Forget your people and your father's house. Let the king be enthralled by your beauty; honor him, for he is your lord. The city of Tyre will come with a gift, people of wealth will seek your favor. All glorious is the princess within her chamber; her gown is interwoven with gold. In embroidered garments she is led to the king; her virgin companions follow her—those brought to be with her. Led in with joy and gladness, they enter the palace of the king. Your sons will take the place of your fathers; you will make them princes throughout the land. I will perpetuate your memory through all generations; therefore the nations will praise you for ever and ever. (Psalm 45)

Our humble, majestic, beautiful, powerful and glorious Bridegroom is enthralled with His Bride! We see that our Jesus is anointed with the oil of joy above all of His companions. He is the happiest and most joyful man that ever lived! Yes, it was, *"for the joy set before Him that He endured the cross"* (see Hebrews 12:2). He paid an unimaginable price for us. And we, in grateful and humble response, are enthralled with Him!

We must not forget what the end of the age is all about. It is about a perfect, eternal, omnipotent, gracious and ever-loving Father presenting His beloved Son—the beautiful, majestic, glorious, enraptured, adoring, warrior Bridegroom King—with His inheritance: the pure, holy, lovely, delightful, enduring, persevering and overcoming Bride. We must not turn aside from the most excellent way (see I Corinthians 12:31-13:1). Let us be encouraged to continue steadfast and press on toward Jesus until He returns.

Therefore, since we are surrounded by such a great cloud of witnesses, let us throw off everything that hinders and the sin that so easily entangles. And let us run with perseverance the race marked out for us, fixing our eyes on Jesus, the pioneer and perfecter of faith. For the joy set before him he endured the cross, scorning its shame, and sat down at the right hand of the throne of God. Consider him who endured such opposition from sinners, so that you will not grow weary and lose heart. (Hebrews 12:1-3)

2 | THE WAY BACK TO EDEN

In the beginning, things were very good! Looking back, we see an image of perfection.

So God created mankind in his own image, in the image of God he created them; male and female he created them. God blessed them and said to them, 'Be fruitful and increase in number; fill the earth and subdue it. Rule over the fish in the sea and the birds in the sky and over every living creature that moves on the ground.' Then God said, 'I give you every seed-bearing plant on the face of the whole earth and every tree that has fruit with seed in it. They will be yours for food. And to all the beasts of the earth and all the birds in the sky and all the creatures that move along the ground—everything that has the breath of life in it—I give every green plant for food.' And it was so. God saw all that he had made, and it was very good. And there was evening, and there was morning—the sixth day. Thus the heavens and the earth were completed in all their vast array. By the seventh day God had finished the work he had been doing; so on the seventh day he rested from all his work. Then God blessed the seventh day and made it holy, because on it he rested from all the work of creating that he had done. (Genesis 1:27-2:3)

Now the Lord God had planted a garden in the east, in Eden; and there he put the man he had formed. The Lord God made all kinds of trees grow out of the ground— trees that were pleasing to the eye and good for food. In the middle of the garden were the tree of life and the tree of the knowledge of good and evil. A river watering the garden flowed from Eden; from there it was separated into four headwaters. The name of the first is the Pishon; it winds through the entire land of Havilah, where there is gold. (The gold of that land is good; aromatic resin and onyx are also there.) The name of the second river is the Gihon; it winds through the entire land of Cush. The name of the third river is the Tigris; it runs along the east side of Ashur. And the fourth river is the Euphrates. The Lord God took the man and put him in the Garden of Eden to work it and take care of it. And the Lord God commanded the man, "You are free to eat from any tree in the garden; but you must not eat from the tree of the knowledge of good and evil, for when you eat from it you will certainly die."

The Lord God said, "It is not good for the man to be alone. I will make a helper suitable for him."

Now the Lord God had formed out of the ground all the wild animals and all the birds in the sky. He brought them to the man to see what he would name them; and whatever the man called each living creature, that was its name. So the man gave names to all the livestock, the birds in the sky and all the wild animals.

But for Adam no suitable helper was found. So the Lord God caused the man to fall into a deep sleep; and while he was sleeping, he took one of the man's ribs and then closed up the place with flesh. Then the Lord God made a woman from the rib he had taken out of the man, and he brought her to the man. The man said, "This is now bone of my bones and flesh of my flesh; she shall be called 'woman,' for she was taken out of man." That is why a man leaves his father and mother and is united to his wife, and they become one flesh. Adam and his wife were both naked, and they felt no shame. (Genesis 2:8-25)

God had created an indescribably beautiful place with wonderful creatures. In this wonderful garden setting, God lovingly placed and a man and a woman, made in His image, to take care of it. He also requested that they honor Him by obeying a few simple commands.

We all know what happened. Adam and Eve violated the love relationship they had with their Creator, failing to comply with God's basic instructions. To Adam and Eve's credit, they had yet to see and experience the devastation that sin causes. This devastation is something that we have seen and experienced now for thousands of years. Therefore, we, of all people, have no excuse! The choice we have set before us is very clear: good vs. evil; life vs. death; man-made rules vs. a love relationship with Father God. Let us choose wisely!

Let us take a high level view of the history of mankind from the point of the fall until the end of the age. Let us also review what God has said is soon to take place in the heavens and on the earth.

The Natural History of Mankind on the Earth

After the Fall

Genesis 3:6-10	
"...she [Eve] took some and ate it...and he [Adam] ate it." *He [Adam] answered, "I heard you in the garden, and I was afraid because I was naked; so I hid."*	Mankind Gives Their God-given Authority on Earth over to Satan
Genesis 3:15 *God: Her [Eve's] offspring "will crush your [Satan's] head, and you will strike his heel."*	Father God Promises that His Beloved Son, Jesus, and His Seed, His Bride—the Church, Will Take the Authority Back from Satan
Revelation 12:11 *"They triumphed over him [Satan] by **the blood of the Lamb** and by the word of their testimony; they did not love their lives so much as to shrink from death."*	Regenerated Mankind, washed by the Blood of the Lamb and empowered by the Spirit of Truth (the Holy Spirit), will conquer Satan! As we welcome Jesus back as our Bridegroom, King and Judge, we will War alongside Him to Kick Satan out and labor with Him to reestablish the Father's Kingdom of Love on the Earth!

After the fall of mankind, our Father God promptly prophesied the destruction of Satan's works and by whom it would come. God had a plan from the beginning; He was looking for a people who would choose to walk with Him in a love relationship—in the Spirit of Life (The Tree of Life). He was looking for a people who would not live and operate in a human-made system of do's and don'ts that is devoid of loving relationship, a system that incubates a spirit of death (The Tree of the Knowledge of Good and Evil). Father God prophesied that His Son, Jesus Christ—the sinless second Adam—would gain victory over Satan, death and the grave! He also prophesied that His overcoming Bride, His Church, would come forth from the sands of time. Through the Blood of the Lamb, Jesus Christ—our Savior, Lord and elder Brother—and by the power of His Holy Spirit, the Bride would also have victory over Satan. For overcoming Satan, the Bride would receive many rewards (see Revelation 2-3 & 20-21).

God told Satan after the fall that Eve's seed, *"will crush [Satan's] head"* and that he would *"strike his heel"* (see Genesis 3:15).

God was prophesying about Jesus, but also about Jesus' seed—His Inheritance, His glorious Bride, His victorious sons and daughters!

Born through Adversity to Face and Overcome Adversity

As I was completing this part of the book, I was wrestling in prayer with the subject of adversity. I felt the Lord leading me to go back to Genesis 3:16.

To the woman he said, "I will make your pains in childbearing very severe; with painful labor you will give birth to children. Your desire will be for your husband, and he will rule over you." (Genesis 3:16)

We know from the account in Genesis that mankind failed after being given management of Eden. It was as if God had handed them paradise on a silver platter. After that initial failure, God laid out a new pattern. Mankind would be born through adversity to face and overcome adversity. Mankind would volunteer, only out of their own free will, to fight alongside their Creator (see Psalm 110:3). Father God and His sons and daughters would fight and overcome evil together. Mankind would overcome with God, through God and for God. Having faced and overcome adversity with God, mankind would then value the Father, the Living Word (His Son) and His paradise. Yes, the final outcome would be that the overcoming sons and daughters (the Bride) would honor the ever-loving Father by greatly desiring the Husband (the Bridegroom). The loving Bridegroom would rule as King over the earth, with His Bride ruling by His side.

But God wouldn't just put the enormous task of facing such great adversity on mankind without first sending His beloved Son as a forerunner to walk it out, to break open the way by laying down His own life for them. He would do this also as an example for His sons and daughters to follow. In return, His sons and daughters (the Bride) would be willing to lay down their lives for their Bridegroom King.

We learn from scripture that Jesus was born by the Holy Spirit (see Luke 1:35). He was born into adverse conditions (see Luke 2, Matthew 2 & Revelation 12). He was able to overcome by also being filled with the Holy Spirit. We actually see this basic pattern in Genesis 3:16, John 3:16 and Matthew 3:16.

I will make your pains in childbearing very severe; with painful labor you will give birth to children. Your desire will be for your husband, and he will rule over you. (Genesis 3:16)

For God so loved the world that he gave his one and only

Son, that whoever believes in him shall not perish but have eternal life. (John 3:16)

As soon as Jesus was baptized, he went up out of the water. At that moment heaven was opened, and he saw the Spirit of God descending like a dove and alighting on him. (Matthew 3:16)

As soon as Jesus was filled with the Holy Spirit, He faced the devil head on (see Matthew 3 & 4). He was faithful to pour out His life as a sacrifice for us, defeating death and the grave on the cross (see Isaiah 53). But what about His inheritance? We see clearly that Jesus was victorious over the enemy. But He had no descendants! It seemed that His inheritance was cut off. The angel Gabriel spoke to Daniel concerning this.

Then after the sixty-two weeks the Messiah will be cut off and have nothing... (Daniel 9:26, NASB)

The prophet Isaiah also prophesied about this issue, but also provided the answer.

He was taken from prison and from judgment, and who will declare His generation? For He was cut off from the land of the living; for the transgressions of My people He was stricken. (Isaiah 53:8, NKJV)

Yet it pleased the Lord to bruise Him; He has put Him to grief. When You make His soul an offering for sin, He shall see His seed, He shall prolong His days, and the pleasure of the Lord shall prosper in His hand. (Isaiah 53:10, NKJV)

His inheritance, His seed, would be supernatural too; they would also be born of the Holy Spirit!

Jesus replied, "Very truly I tell you, no one can see the kingdom of God unless they are born again." "How can someone be born when they are old?" Nicodemus asked. "Surely they cannot enter a second time into their mother's womb to be born!" Jesus answered, "Very truly I tell you, no one can enter the kingdom of God unless they are born of water and the Spirit. Flesh gives birth to flesh, but the Spirit gives birth to spirit. You should not be surprised at my saying, 'You must be born again.' The wind blows wherever it pleases. You hear its sound, but you cannot tell where it comes from or where it is going. So it is with everyone born of the Spirit." (John 3:3-8)

Yet to all who did receive him, to those who believed in his name, he gave the right to become children of God— children born not of natural descent, nor of human decision or a husband's will, but born of God. (John 1:12-13)

Jesus also instructed us to be filled with the Holy Spirit, just as He had been.

Jesus said, "But you will receive power when the Holy Spirit comes on you; and you will be my witnesses in Jerusalem, and in all Judea and Samaria, and to the ends of the earth." (Acts 1:8)

Therefore, the Father planned for His Son, Jesus, to be born of a virgin by the Holy Spirit and then to be filled with the Holy Spirit. Filled with the Holy Spirit, He would face the enemy, even unto death, and defeat Him! The Father also planned for His sons and daughters to be "born again" by the Holy Spirit (made possible by the Blood of the Lamb) and then to be filled with the Holy Spirit. Filled with the Holy Spirit, they would also face the enemy, even at the risk of death, and defeat him!

So, we can clearly see that we are called to labor with Jesus in finishing His work.

And he said, "The Son of Man must suffer many things and be rejected by the elders, the chief priests and the teachers of the law, and he must be killed and on the third day be raised to life." Then he said to them all: "Whoever wants to be my disciple must deny themselves and take up their cross daily and follow me. For whoever wants to save their life will lose it, but whoever loses their life for me will save it. What good is it for someone to gain the whole world, and yet lose or forfeit their very self? Whoever is ashamed of me and my words, the Son of Man will be ashamed of them when he comes in his glory and in the glory of the Father and of the holy angels." (Luke 9:22-26)

The Birth of the Kingdom of God on the Earth

In the same way that Jesus and each individual follower of Christ is born into this world, so will it be with the birth of Kingdom of God at the end of the age. The Kingdom of God will be ushered in during a time of a great outpouring of the Holy Spirit. The Church will face great adversity. Filled with the power of the Holy Spirit, the Church will overcome! And the desire of the Bride (the Church) will be for the Bridegroom. The Bride will call out to Him until He returns. Joel 2:28-32 gives a great synopsis of this time.

The Day of the Lord

"And afterward, I will pour out my Spirit on all people. Your sons and daughters will prophesy, your old men will dream dreams, your young men will see visions. Even on my servants, both men and women, I will pour out my Spirit in those days. I will show wonders in the heavens and on the earth, blood and fire and billows of smoke. The sun will be turned to darkness and the moon to blood before the coming of the great and dreadful day of the Lord. And everyone who calls on the name of the Lord will be saved; for on Mount Zion and in Jerusalem there will be deliverance, as the Lord has said, even among the survivors whom the Lord calls." (Joel 2:28-32)

We also see a prophetic picture of this time in Haggai.

But now be strong, Zerubbabel,' declares the Lord. 'Be strong, Joshua son of Jozadak, the high priest. Be strong, all you people of the land,' declares the Lord, 'and work. For I am with you,' declares the Lord Almighty. 'This is what I covenanted with you when you came out of Egypt. And my Spirit remains among you. Do not fear.' "This is what the Lord Almighty says: 'In a little while I will once more shake the heavens and the earth, the sea and the dry land. I will shake all nations, and what is desired by all nations will come, and I will fill this house with glory,' says the Lord Almighty. 'The silver is mine and the gold is mine,' declares the Lord Almighty. 'The glory of this present house will be greater than the glory of the former house,' says the Lord Almighty. 'And in this place I will grant peace,' declares the Lord Almighty." (Haggai 2:4-9)

Now, let us go back and review Genesis 3:16 once again.

To the woman he said, "I will make your pains in childbearing very severe; with painful labor you will give birth to children. Your desire will be for your husband, and he will rule over you." (Genesis 3:16)

The woman (the Church) will give birth to her children in the severe pain of labor. And the desire of the Church, the Bride, will be for her husband, the Bridegroom—Jesus Christ. And He will rule over Her, as well as the whole earth!

We know from scriptures throughout the Word of God that the end of the age, the birth of His Kingdom on the earth, will be the greatest time of adversity the world has ever known. Jesus also tells us that it will be preceded by birth pains.

"You will hear of wars and rumors of wars, but see to it that you are not alarmed. Such things must happen, but the end is still to come. Nation will rise against nation, and kingdom against kingdom. There will be famines and earthquakes in various places. All these are the beginning of birth pains." (Matthew 24:6-8)

"For then there will be great distress, unequaled from the beginning of the world until now—and never to be equaled again. If those days had not been cut short, no one would survive, but for the sake of the elect those days will be shortened." (Matthew 24:21-22)

How can we describe the birth of a child? Couldn't we call it beautiful and terrible—terrible and beautiful? It is extremely painful, emotional, traumatic, messy and even bloody! But the pain and adversity, though terrible and intense, are quickly gone. What remains is beautiful and magnificent indeed!

But why is this painful, terrible and intense process necessary for the birth of the Kingdom on the earth? I think we find a key to this mystery in Hosea. Here we find a description of the bonding process that happens during the labor at the end of the age.

Therefore I am now going to allure her; I will lead her into the wilderness and speak tenderly to her. There I will give her back her vineyards, and will make the Valley of Achor a door of hope. There she will respond as in the days of her youth, as in the day she came up out of Egypt. In that day," declares the Lord, "you will call me 'my husband'; you will no longer call me 'my master.' I will remove the names of the Baals from her lips; no longer will their names be invoked. In that day I will make a covenant for them with the beasts of the field, the birds in the sky and the creatures that move along the ground. Bow and sword and battle I will abolish from the land, so that all may lie down in safety. I will betroth you to me forever; I will betroth you in righteousness and justice, in love and compassion. I will betroth you in faithfulness, and you will acknowledge the Lord." (Hosea 2:13-20)

In the book of Revelation, we see another prophetic picture of the woman, the Church, fleeing into the wilderness to be cared for by God. We also see a foreshadowing of this when Jesus was an infant and had to be carried by Joseph and Mary into the desert of Egypt for several years in order to protect Jesus' life.

When the dragon saw that he had been hurled to the

earth, he pursued the woman who had given birth to the male child. The woman was given the two wings of a great eagle, so that she might fly to the place prepared for her in the wilderness, where she would be taken care of for a time, times and half a time, out of the serpent's reach. Then from his mouth the serpent spewed water like a river, to overtake the woman and sweep her away with the torrent. But the earth helped the woman by opening its mouth and swallowing the river that the dragon had spewed out of his mouth. Then the dragon was enraged at the woman and went off to wage war against the rest of her offspring—those who keep God's commands and hold fast their testimony about Jesus. (Revelation 12:13-17)

As we saw in Hosea, during the labor process, the people of God will cry out to Him—and He will answer! He will speak tenderly to them and they, the Bride, will begin to call Jesus their "Husband." We also get another picture of this in Zechariah.

Mourning for the One They Pierced

"And I will pour out on the house of David and the inhabitants of Jerusalem a spirit of grace and supplication. They will look on me, the one they have pierced, and they will mourn for him as one mourns for an only child, and grieve bitterly for him as one grieves for a firstborn son. On that day the weeping in Jerusalem will be as great as the weeping of Hadad Rimmon in the plain of Megiddo. The land will mourn, each clan by itself, with their wives by themselves: the clan of the house of David and their wives, the clan of the house of Nathan and their wives, the clan of the house of Levi and

their wives, the clan of Shimei and their wives, and all the rest of the clans and their wives." (Zechariah 12:10-14)

But someone may ask, "Isn't this just happening in Israel, or only in Jerusalem?" Jesus provides the answer. He said, *"For it will come on all those who live on the face of the whole earth"* (see Luke 21:35). We also see further clarification in the book of Revelation. It appears that whole Bride of Christ—followers of Christ from every tribe, tongue and nation—will experience this beautiful and terrible birthing process.

After this I looked, and there before me was a great multitude that no one could count, from every nation, tribe, people and language, standing before the throne and before the Lamb. They were wearing white robes and were holding palm branches in their hands...

...Then one of the elders asked me, "These in white robes—who are they, and where did they come from?" I answered, "Sir, you know." And he said, "These are they who have come out of the great tribulation; they have washed their robes and made them white in the blood of the Lamb. Therefore, "they are before the throne of God and serve him day and night in his temple; and he who sits on the throne will shelter them with his presence. 'Never again will they hunger; never again will they thirst. The sun will not beat down on them,' nor any scorching heat. For the Lamb at the center of the throne will be their shepherd; 'he will lead them to springs of living water.' 'And God will wipe away every tear from their eyes.'" (Revelation 7:9,13-17)

In the book of Isaiah we also see a prophetic picture of the global impact of this historic and cataclysmic time.

See, the Lord is going to lay waste the earth and devastate it; he will ruin its face and scatter its inhabitants—it will be the same for priest as for people, for the master as for his servant, for the mistress as for her servant, for seller as for buyer, for borrower as for lender, for debtor as for creditor. The earth will be completely laid waste and totally plundered. The Lord has spoken this word. (Isaiah 24:1-3)

But the good news is, as Jesus promised, the pain of labor will be over quickly. The Bride will overcome and Jesus will return! We will behold Him in His glory, strength and beauty!

"They triumphed over him [Satan] by the blood of the Lamb and by the word of their testimony; they did not love their lives so much as to shrink from death. Therefore rejoice, you heavens and you who dwell in them! But woe to the earth and the sea, because the devil has gone down to you! He is filled with fury, because he knows that his time is short." (Revelation 12:11-12)

"There will be signs in the sun, moon and stars. On the earth, nations will be in anguish and perplexity at the roaring and tossing of the sea. People will faint from terror, apprehensive of what is coming on the world, for the heavenly bodies will be shaken. At that time they will see the Son of Man coming in a cloud with power and great glory. When these things begin to take place, stand up and lift up your heads, because your redemption is drawing near." (Luke 21:25-28)

Let us encourage one another with Jesus' promise, *"To the one who is victorious, I will give the right to sit with me on my throne, just as I was victorious and sat down with my Father on his throne. Whoever has ears, let them hear what the Spirit says to the churches"* (Revelation 3:21-22).

It is Our Time in History

So, for those of us who have decided to walk in God's love and in obedience to Him, it is important to understand our place in history and what He expects of us. We were born into the most exciting time in human history! We were hand-picked and specifically chosen to be alive during this time. Congratulations are in order! *What a privilege it is to be alive right now!* Through Jesus Christ, you have the ability to overcome Satan and to help kick him off of the earth; and you will receive all of the rewards of the overcomer for doing so.

So, as we approach the very end of the age, we are at the moment of preparation. We are being prepared by the Lord to cross the Jordan river and to head back into Eden. The Lord is encouraging us at the river's banks. The Lord is calling for His end time warriors to arise, shine and take back the land! He says, *"Be strong and courageous. Do not be afraid or terrified because of them, for the Lord your God goes with you; he will never leave you nor forsake you"* (Deuteronomy 31:6). The Captain of the Host will go before us and lead the way. As it happened in the days of Joshua (see Joshua 3:13-15), it will happen again!

> *"The One who breaks open the way will go up before them; they will break through the gate and go out. Their King will pass through before them, the Lord at their head." (Micah 2:13)*

"The gatekeeper opens the gate for him, and the sheep listen to his voice. He calls his own sheep by name and leads them out. When he has brought out all his own, he goes on ahead of them, and his sheep follow him because they know his voice. But they will never follow a stranger; in fact, they will run away from him because they do not recognize a stranger's voice." (John 10:3-5)

The Lord is my shepherd, I lack nothing. He makes me lie down in green pastures, he leads me beside quiet waters, he refreshes my soul. He guides me along the right paths for his name's sake. Even though I walk through the darkest valley, I will fear no evil, for you are with me; your rod and your staff, they comfort me. You prepare a table before me in the presence of my enemies. You anoint my head with oil; my cup overflows. Surely your goodness and love will follow me all the days of my life, and I will dwell in the house of the Lord forever. (Psalm 23)

During this time of preparation, He will blow upon us with His wind and pour upon us the Holy fire of His presence. He will do this to prepare our hearts and minds for what is coming, including uprooting our worldly thought patterns and habits of living. As the Holy Spirit and fire come upon us, we will go out and prepare the way for the Lord's return!

"I have come to bring fire on the earth, and how I wish it were already kindled!" (John 12:49)

The Father's ultimate desire and purpose for the end of the age is to present His beloved Son with His inheritance— His glorious Bride! We will overcome Satan and uproot his kingdom by the blood of the Lamb and by the power of the

Holy Spirit! Jesus will come back to battle alongside us to finish His work. Then He will take us back to the garden, so we can walk and fellowship with Him in the cool of the day. We will rule and reign with Him in His Kingdom of Love and Holiness, just as He originally intended!

3 | THE RIVER OF WATER AND FIRE

In the beginning there was a river that watered the Garden of Eden.

A river watering the garden flowed from Eden; from there it was separated into four headwaters. The name of the first is the Pishon; it winds through the entire land of Havilah, where there is gold. (The gold of that land is good; aromatic resin and onyx are also there.) (Genesis 2:10-12)

The Word of God prophesies that this river will return, once again bringing life to the earth. What is flowing in and from His river, and what it accomplishes on the earth, reveals to us what is in the Father's heart.

"The poor and needy search for water, but there is none; their tongues are parched with thirst. But I the Lord will answer them; I, the God of Israel, will not forsake them. I will make rivers flow on barren heights, and springs within the valleys. I will turn the desert into pools of

water, and the parched ground into springs. I will put in the desert the cedar and the acacia, the myrtle and the olive. I will set junipers in the wasteland, the fir and the cypress together, so that people may see and know, may consider and understand, that the hand of the Lord has done this, that the Holy One of Israel has created it." (Isaiah 41:17-20)

"How beautiful are your tents, Jacob, your dwelling places, Israel! Like valleys they spread out, like gardens beside a river, like aloes planted by the Lord, like cedars beside the waters. Water will flow from their buckets; their seed will have abundant water." (Numbers 24:5-7)

There is a river whose streams make glad the city of God, the holy place where the Most High dwells. God is within her, she will not fall; God will help her at break of day. Nations are in uproar, kingdoms fall; he lifts his voice, the earth melts. The Lord Almighty is with us; the God of Jacob is our fortress. (Psalm 46:4-7)

But let justice roll on like a river, righteousness like a never-failing stream! (Amos 5:24)

For this is what the Lord says: "I will extend peace to her like a river, and the wealth of nations like a flooding stream; you will nurse and be carried on her arm and dandled on her knees. As a mother comforts her child, so will I comfort you; and you will be comforted over Jerusalem." (Isaiah 66:12-13)

Right now, we know that this life-giving river exists in heaven; Daniel saw the river in a vision.

"As I looked, 'thrones were set in place, and the Ancient of Days took his seat. His clothing was as white as snow; the hair of his head was white like wool. His throne was flaming with fire, and its wheels were all ablaze. A river of fire was flowing, coming out from before him. Thousands upon thousands attended him; ten thousand times ten thousand stood before him. The court was seated, and the books were opened.'" (Daniel 7:9-10)

What do we do about this river? We know the river existed in Eden. We know that the river exists in heaven. But, we want the river to come back to the earth, don't we? Jesus instructed us to pray to the Father to ask Him to bring it back to earth!

"This, then, is how you should pray: 'Our Father in heaven, hallowed be your name, your kingdom come, your will be done, on earth as it is in heaven.'" (Matthew 6:9-10)

But, this river, it is spiritual or physical? Is it water, or is it fire? I firmly believe the answer is, *"Yes!"* It is both spiritual and physical; and it is both water and fire. Undoubtedly, it also has attributes that are beyond our comprehension.

We can see "spiritual water" aspects of this river in the gospel of John.

On the last and greatest day of the festival, Jesus stood and said in a loud voice, "Let anyone who is thirsty come to me and drink. Whoever believes in me, as Scripture has said, rivers of living water will flow from within them." (John 7:37-38)

We can also see some of the "physical water" attributes of

31

the river that is coming to the earth in the book of Ezekiel. Many of these physical attributes mirror spiritual attributes as well. As the apostle Paul put it, this is, *"...the mystery of his will according to his good pleasure, which he purposed in Christ, to be put into effect when the times reach their fulfillment—to bring unity to all things in heaven and on earth under Christ"* (Ephesians 1:7).

The River From the Temple

The man brought me back to the entrance to the temple, and I saw water coming out from under the threshold of the temple toward the east (for the temple faced east). The water was coming down from under the south side of the temple, south of the altar. He then brought me out through the north gate and led me around the outside to the outer gate facing east, and the water was trickling from the south side.

As the man went eastward with a measuring line in his hand, he measured off a thousand cubits and then led me through water that was ankle-deep. He measured off another thousand cubits and led me through water that was knee-deep. He measured off another thousand and led me through water that was up to the waist. He measured off another thousand, but now it was a river that I could not cross, because the water had risen and was deep enough to swim in—a river that no one could cross. He asked me, "Son of man, do you see this?"

Then he led me back to the bank of the river. When I arrived there, I saw a great number of trees on each side of the river. He said to me, "This water flows toward the eastern region and goes down into the Arabah, where it enters the Dead Sea. When it empties into the sea, the salty water there becomes fresh. Swarms of living creatures will live wherever the river flows. There will be large numbers of fish, because this water flows there and makes the salt water fresh; so where the river flows everything will live. Fishermen will stand along the shore; from En Gedi to En Eglaim there will be places for spreading nets. The fish will be of many kinds—like the fish of the Mediterranean Sea. But the swamps and marshes will not become fresh; they will be left for salt. Fruit trees of all kinds will grow on both banks of the river. Their leaves will not wither, nor will their fruit fail. Every month they will bear fruit, because the water from the sanctuary flows to them. Their fruit will serve for food and their leaves for healing." (Ezekiel 47:1-12)

Even today, we know living waters flow from our hearts when we are filled with the Holy Spirit. And we know that we should pray for what is in heaven to come to earth. But when will we see the total reality of heaven coming to earth that Paul talked about in is his letter to the Ephesians? And when will the river that is in heaven actually return to earth? Zechariah provided the answer. The river will finally return and manifest itself on the earth when the Lord's prayer is finally answered in fullness—during the Day of the Lord!

The Lord Comes and Reigns

A day of the Lord is coming, Jerusalem, when your possessions will be plundered and divided up within your very walls. I will gather all the nations to Jerusalem to fight against it; the city will be captured, the houses ransacked, and the women raped. Half of the city will go into exile, but the rest of the people will not be taken from the city. Then the Lord will go out and fight against those nations, as he fights on a day of battle. On that day his feet will stand on the Mount of Olives, east of Jerusalem, and the Mount of Olives will be split in two from east to west, forming a great valley, with half of the mountain moving north and half moving south. You will flee by my mountain valley, for it will extend to Azel. You will flee as you fled from the earthquake in the days of Uzziah king of Judah. Then the Lord my God will come, and all the holy ones with him. On that day there will be neither sunlight nor cold, frosty darkness. It will be a unique day—a day known only to the Lord—with no distinction between day and night. When evening comes, there will be light. On that day living water will flow out from Jerusalem, half of it east to the Dead Sea and half of it west to the Mediterranean Sea, in summer and in winter. The Lord will be king over the whole earth. On that day there will be one Lord, and his name the only name. The whole land, from Geba to Rimmon, south of Jerusalem, will become like the Arabah. But Jerusalem will be raised up high from the Benjamin Gate to the site of the First Gate, to the Corner Gate, and from the Tower of Hananel to the royal winepresses, and will remain in its place. It will be inhabited; never again will it be destroyed. Jerusalem will be secure. (Zechariah 14:1-11)

We see that the river will return at the time when Jerusalem will become a praise in all the earth—when the Lord returns to rule from His throne in the Holy City!

This is what Isaiah son of Amoz saw concerning Judah and Jerusalem: In the last days the mountain of the Lord's temple will be established as the highest of the mountains; it will be exalted above the hills, and all nations will stream to it. Many peoples will come and say, "Come, let us go up to the mountain of the Lord, to the temple of the God of Jacob. He will teach us his ways, so that we may walk in his paths." The law will go out from Zion, the word of the Lord from Jerusalem. (Isaiah 2:1-3)

"In the time of those kings, the God of heaven will set up a kingdom that will never be destroyed, nor will it be left to another people. It will crush all those kingdoms and bring them to an end, but it will itself endure forever. This is the meaning of the vision of the rock cut out of a mountain, but not by human hands—a rock that broke the iron, the bronze, the clay, the silver and the gold to pieces. The great God has shown the king what will take place in the future. The dream is true and its interpretation is trustworthy." (Daniel 2:44-45)

The River of Purifying Fire

As we can see, the river returns to the earth in the context of a mighty conflict. During the years leading up to when the river returns, there is a cleansing taking place on the earth. Now we also see the river as fire that purifies and refines.

Who can withstand his indignation? Who can endure his fierce anger? His wrath is poured out like fire; the rocks are shattered before him. (Nahum 1:6)

But who can endure the day of his coming? Who can stand when he appears? For he will be like a refiner's fire or a launderer's soap. (Malachi 3:2)

See, I have refined you, though not as silver; I have tested *you in the furnace of affliction. For my own sake, for my own sake, I do this. How can I let myself be defamed? I will not yield my glory to another. (Isaiah 48:10-11)*

"Jacob will be a fire and Joseph a flame; Esau will be stubble, and they will set him on fire and destroy him. There will be no survivors from Esau." The Lord has spoken. (Obadiah 1:18)

If anyone builds on this foundation using gold, silver, costly stones, wood, hay or straw, their work will be shown for what it is, because the Day will bring it to light. It will be revealed with fire, and the fire will test the quality of each person's work. If what has been built survives, the builder will receive a reward. If it is burned up, the builder will suffer loss but yet will be saved— even though only as one escaping through the flames. (I Corinthians 3:12-15)

The Lord will pour out His refining fire on the earth to cleanse and liberate it from sin and oppression, and to bring purity to His people. At the same time, He will be a *"wall of fire"* around His beloved remnant to protect them (see Zechariah 2:5).

I consider that our present sufferings are not worth comparing with the glory that will be revealed in us. For the creation waits in eager expectation for the children of God to be revealed. For the creation was subjected to frustration, not by its own choice, but by the will of the one who subjected it, in hope that the creation itself will be liberated from its bondage to decay and brought into the freedom and glory of the children of God. We know that the whole creation has been groaning as in the pains of childbirth right up to the present time. (Romans 8:18-22)

He will cleanse the bloodstains from Jerusalem by a spirit of judgment and a spirit of fire. Then the Lord will create over all of Mount Zion and over those who assemble there a cloud of smoke by day and a glow of flaming fire by night; over all the glory will be a canopy. It will be a shelter and shade from the heat of the day, and a refuge and hiding place from the storm and rain. (Isaiah 4:4-6)

"Neither their silver nor their gold will be able to save them on the day of the Lord's wrath. In the fire of his jealousy the whole earth will be consumed, for he will make a sudden end of all who live on the earth." (Zephaniah 1:18)

This is astounding! Everyone will die?! But, we know from scripture that this is a broad and general statement; it does not mean every single person will die. Instead, we know there will be a remnant that remains on the earth.

See, the day of the Lord is coming—a cruel day, with wrath and fierce anger—to make the land desolate and destroy the sinners within it. The stars of heaven and their constellations will not show their light. The rising sun will be darkened and the moon will not give its light. I will punish the world for its evil, the wicked for their sins. I will put an end to the arrogance of the haughty and will humble the pride of the ruthless. I will make people scarcer than pure gold, more rare than the gold of Ophir [See Psalm 45:9]. Therefore I will make the heavens tremble; and the earth will shake from its place at the wrath of the Lord Almighty, in the day of his burning anger. *(Isaiah 13:9-13)*

Surely the Lord does nothing without first telling His friends, the prophets (see Amos 3:7). Throughout the Bible, we see various aspects of this incredible scene described. The following are but a few more examples.

"Surely the day is coming; it will burn like a furnace. All the arrogant and every evildoer will be stubble, and the day that is coming will set them on fire," says the Lord Almighty. "Not a root or a branch will be left to them. But for you who revere my name, the sun of righteousness will rise with healing in its rays. And you will go out and frolic like well-fed calves. Then you will trample on the wicked; they will be ashes under the soles of your feet on the day when I act," says the Lord Almighty. (Malachi 4:1-3)

"Do not fear, for I have redeemed you; I have summoned you by name; you are mine. When you pass through the waters, I will be with you; and when you pass through the rivers, they will not sweep over you. When you walk through the fire, you will not be burned; the flames will not set you ablaze. For I am the Lord your God, the Holy One of Israel, your Savior." (Isaiah 43:1-3)

This is what the Lord Almighty says: "I am very jealous for Zion; I am burning with jealousy for her." This is what the Lord says: "I will return to Zion and dwell in Jerusalem. Then Jerusalem will be called the Faithful City, and the mountain of the Lord Almighty will be called the Holy Mountain." (Zechariah 8:2-3)

While the angel who was speaking to me was leaving, another angel came to meet him and said to him: "Run, tell that young man, 'Jerusalem will be a city without walls because of the great number of people and animals in it. And I myself will be a wall of fire around it,' declares the Lord, 'and I will be its glory within.'"
(Zechariah 2:3-5)

Once the river of fire completes the process of purifying and liberating the whole earth from sin and oppression, the river of water will physically appear in Jerusalem and begin doing its work to renew and bring life back to the earth; it will even bring the Dead Sea back to life! The river will begin to bring healing to the nations.

We don't know exactly how long the earth's restoration will take. However, we do know that in the book of Revelation, John speaks of a one thousand year period, commonly known as the millennium (see Revelation 20:1-7), where our prayers will finally be answered and the word of the Lord spoken through the prophets will be vindicated in fullness. During this time, Eden will begin to return to the earth. We will finally have "peace on earth" (see Luke 2:14) and the Father's goodwill towards mankind will be on full, glorious display for all to see! The wicked and murderous will be no more. The nations will come to worship Jesus in Jerusalem!

"On the day I cleanse you from all your sins, I will resettle your towns, and the ruins will be rebuilt. The desolate land will be cultivated instead of lying desolate in the sight of all who pass through it. They will say, "This land that was laid waste has become like the garden of Eden; the cities that were lying in ruins, desolate and destroyed, are now fortified and inhabited."

"Then the nations around you that remain will know that I the Lord have rebuilt what was destroyed and have replanted what was desolate. I the Lord have spoken, and I will do it.'" (Ezekiel 36:33-36)

Then the survivors from all the nations that have attacked Jerusalem will go up year after year to worship the King, the Lord Almighty, and to celebrate the Festival of Tabernacles. If any of the peoples of the earth do not go up to Jerusalem to worship the King, the Lord Almighty, they will have no rain. (Zechariah 14:16-17)

During and after the millennium, the heavenly and spiritual dimensions of this river will begin to escalate to levels we cannot now fully comprehend, as the natural and spiritual come together under Christ (see Ephesians 1:7). When we come to the end of millennium, there will no longer be any sea (see Revelation 21:1).

Eden Restored

Then the angel showed me the river of the water of life, as clear as crystal, flowing from the throne of God and of the Lamb down the middle of the great street of the city. On each side of the river stood the tree of life, bearing twelve crops of fruit, yielding its fruit every month. And the leaves of the tree are for the healing of the nations. No longer will there be any curse. The throne of God and of the Lamb will be in the city, and his servants will serve him. They will see his face, and his name will be on their foreheads. There will be no more night. They will not need the light of a lamp or the light of the sun, for the Lord God will give them light. And they will reign for ever and ever. (Revelation 22:1-5)

Where Are We Now?

I believe we are now living in a time, spiritually speaking, where the river is approaching knee deep. The river, just like Ezekiel saw, is growing deeper and deeper. We are not entering a time of spiritual renewal or revival such as we've seen in the past, where it appears and then dies down again. Instead, we are entering the time that Ezekiel saw, where the river will grow deeper and deeper until we are swimming in it! It will continue to grow deeper until the time that it fully materializes on the earth. We are entering a time of fullness—the fullness of time. As we enter this time, we must stay in the river. In the river, there is life! Outside of the river there is only increasing darkness, death and destruction. As we well know, without Jesus, the source of living water, we can do nothing!

> "...whoever drinks the water I give them will never thirst. Indeed, the water I give them will become in them a spring of water welling up to eternal life." (John 4:14)

> "I am the vine; you are the branches. If you remain in me and I in you, you will bear much fruit; apart from me you can do nothing." (John 15:5)

So, let us stay in His river and contend for its complete manifestation until Jesus returns. Let us also pray that His Holy Spirit and fire burn out anything from our hearts that He does not find desirable. Let our hearts be a resting place for His consuming fire. In these increasingly dark days, let us then be a burning bush, a light for all to see, as the manifest glory of the Lord rests upon us. Let many be drawn to the light and may we lead them to their Bridegroom and King!

4 | REDEMPTIVE, MERCIFUL JUDGMENTS VS. THE WRATH OF GOD

How great is the mercy of our Lord! His generosity, kindness, patience and longsuffering are unfathomable to us, inconceivable in our limited and weakened minds. We do not have a full revelation of His divine attributes, because now we only see in part.

For now we see only a reflection as in a mirror; then we shall see face to face. Now I know in part; then I shall know fully, even as I am fully known. (I Corinthians 13:12)

Let us look to Jesus for revelation regarding the depths of His great generosity. Let us ask the Holy Spirit for help as we read the parable of the workers in the vineyard.

"For the kingdom of heaven is like a landowner who went out early in the morning to hire workers for his vineyard. He agreed to pay them a denarius for the day and sent them into his vineyard.

"About nine in the morning he went out and saw others standing in the marketplace doing nothing. He told them, 'You also go and work in my vineyard, and I will pay you whatever is right.' So they went.

"He went out again about noon and about three in the afternoon and did the same thing. About five in the afternoon he went out and found still others standing around. He asked them, 'Why have you been standing here all day long doing nothing?' 'Because no one has hired us,' they answered. He said to them, 'You also go and work in my vineyard.'

"When evening came, the owner of the vineyard said to his foreman, 'Call the workers and pay them their wages, beginning with the last ones hired and going on to the first.' The workers who were hired about five in the afternoon came and each received a denarius. So when those came who were hired first, they expected to receive more. But each one of them also received a denarius. When they received it, they began to grumble against the landowner. 'These who were hired last worked only one hour,' they said, 'and you have made them equal to us who have borne the burden of the work and the heat of the day.'

"But he answered one of them, 'I am not being unfair to you, friend. Didn't you agree to work for a denarius? Take your pay and go. I want to give the one who was hired last the same as I gave you. Don't I have the right to do what I want with my own money? Or are you envious because I am generous?'

"So the last will be first, and the first will be last." (Matthew 20:1-16)

As we well know, Jesus is the Good Shepherd. Jesus said that He came to *"seek and save the lost"* (see Luke 19:10).

The Good Shepherd and His Sheep

"Very truly I tell you Pharisees, anyone who does not enter the sheep pen by the gate, but climbs in by some other way, is a thief and a robber. The one who enters by the gate is the shepherd of the sheep. The gatekeeper opens the gate for him, and the sheep listen to his voice. He calls his own sheep by name and leads them out. When he has brought out all his own, he goes on ahead of them, and his sheep follow him because they know his voice. But they will never follow a stranger; in fact, they will run away from him because they do not recognize a stranger's voice." Jesus used this figure of speech, but the Pharisees did not understand what he was telling them.

Therefore Jesus said again, "Very truly I tell you, I am the gate for the sheep. All who have come before me are thieves and robbers, but the sheep have not listened to them. I am the gate; whoever enters through me will be saved. They will come in and go out, and find pasture. The thief comes only to steal and kill and destroy; I have come that they may have life, and have it to the full."

"I am the good shepherd. The good shepherd lays down his life for the sheep. The hired hand is not the shepherd and does not own the sheep. So when he sees the wolf coming, he abandons the sheep and runs away. Then the wolf attacks the flock and scatters it. The man runs away because he is a hired hand and cares nothing for the sheep. I am the good shepherd; I know my sheep and my sheep know me—just as the Father knows me and I know the Father—and I lay down my life for the sheep. I

have other sheep that are not of this sheep pen. I must bring them also. They too will listen to my voice, and there shall be one flock and one shepherd. The reason my Father loves me is that I lay down my life—only to take it up again. No one takes it from me, but I lay it down of my own accord. I have authority to lay it down and authority to take it up again. This command I received from my Father." (John 10:1-18)

Jesus and His Father have been working passionately at shepherding their people for a long time.

"My Father is always at his work to this very day, and I too am working." (John 5:16)

The Lord Will Be Israel's Shepherd

The word of the Lord came to me: "Son of man, prophesy against the shepherds of Israel; prophesy and say to them: 'This is what the Sovereign Lord says: Woe to you shepherds of Israel who only take care of yourselves! Should not shepherds take care of the flock? You eat the curds, clothe yourselves with the wool and slaughter the choice animals, but you do not take care of the flock. You have not strengthened the weak or healed the sick or bound up the injured. You have not brought back the strays or searched for the lost. You have ruled them harshly and brutally. So they were scattered because there was no shepherd, and when they were scattered they became food for all the wild animals. My sheep wandered over all the mountains and on every high hill. They were scattered over the whole earth, and no one searched or looked for them.'

"'Therefore, you shepherds, hear the word of the Lord: As

surely as I live, declares the Sovereign Lord, because my flock lacks a shepherd and so has been plundered and has become food for all the wild animals, and because my shepherds did not search for my flock but cared for themselves rather than for my flock, therefore, you shepherds, hear the word of the Lord: This is what the Sovereign Lord says: I am against the shepherds and will hold them accountable for my flock. I will remove them from tending the flock so that the shepherds can no longer feed themselves. I will rescue my flock from their mouths, and it will no longer be food for them.

"'For this is what the Sovereign Lord says: I myself will search for my sheep and look after them. As a shepherd looks after his scattered flock when he is with them, so will I look after my sheep. I will rescue them from all the places where they were scattered on a day of clouds and darkness. I will bring them out from the nations and gather them from the countries, and I will bring them into their own land. I will pasture them on the mountains of Israel, in the ravines and in all the settlements in the land. I will tend them in a good pasture, and the mountain heights of Israel will be their grazing land. There they will lie down in good grazing land, and there they will feed in a rich pasture on the mountains of Israel. I myself will tend my sheep and have them lie down, declares the Sovereign Lord. I will search for the lost and bring back the strays. I will bind up the injured and strengthen the weak, but the sleek and the strong I will destroy. I will shepherd the flock with justice.'" (Ezekiel 34:1-16)

Jesus is working to destroy the works of Satan and to bring the lost into His Kingdom. Will we participate with

Him? Are we working with Him or against Him? He greatly desires that we join Him!

> *The one who does what is sinful is of the devil, because the devil has been sinning from the beginning. The reason the Son of God appeared was to destroy the devil's work. (I John 3:8)*

> *Then Jesus came to them and said, "All authority in heaven and on earth has been given to me. Therefore go and make disciples of all nations, baptizing them in the name of the Father and of the Son and of the Holy Spirit, and teaching them to obey everything I have commanded you. And surely I am with you always, to the very end of the age." (Matthew 28:18-20)*

> *And God raised us up with Christ and seated us with him in the heavenly realms in Christ Jesus, in order that in the coming ages he might show the incomparable riches of his grace, expressed in his kindness to us in Christ Jesus. For it is by grace you have been saved, through faith—and this is not from yourselves, it is the gift of God—not by works, so that no one can boast. For we are God's handiwork, created in Christ Jesus to do good works, which God prepared in advance for us to do. (Ephesians 2:6-10)*

> *You, dear children, are from God and have overcome them, because the One who is in you is greater than the one who is in the world. (I John 4:4)*

Jesus is the Lord of the harvest. And He has a great harvest to bring in!

Then He said to His disciples, "The harvest is indeed plentiful, but the laborers are few. So pray to the Lord of the harvest to force out and thrust laborers into His harvest." (Matthew 9:37-38, AMP)

Some of us may be tempted to wonder what is taking Jesus so long to return. The truth is that He is very patient with His harvest, because He doesn't want to lose any of us.

The Lord is not slow in keeping his promise, as some understand slowness. Instead he is patient with you, not wanting anyone to perish, but everyone to come to repentance. (2 Peter 3:9)

How could Jesus maximize His harvest? This is a mystery to be sure. But we do have some clues. Have you ever noticed that the harvest during the flood of Noah's time was very small? To say the least. In fact, there was practically no harvest at all! However, by the grace of God, the people were warned. Although they were warned, they did not listen. However, they didn't get a little bit of rain to show them that water might actually come in larger quantities later. No, when the floods came, they came all at once! It was a complete cleansing of the earth from evil. Now, let's look at the end of the age. Jesus says it is as *"in the days of Noah"* in regards to how the people are living and acting.

"Just as it was in the days of Noah, so also will it be in the days of the Son of Man. People were eating, drinking, marrying and being given in marriage up to the day Noah entered the ark. Then the flood came and destroyed them all. It was the same in the days of Lot. People were eating and drinking, buying and selling, planting and building. But the day Lot left Sodom, fire

and sulfur rained down from heaven and destroyed them all. It will be just like this on the day the Son of Man is revealed. On that day no one who is on the housetop, with possessions inside, should go down to get them. Likewise, no one in the field should go back for anything. Remember Lot's wife! Whoever tries to keep their life will lose it, and whoever loses their life will preserve it. I tell you, on that night two people will be in one bed; one will be taken and the other left. Two women will be grinding grain together; one will be taken and the other left." "Where, Lord?" they asked. He replied, "Where there is a dead body, there the vultures will gather." (Luke 17:26-37)

So, we see that each individual is being warned that their demise may come at any time. Jesus is warning each of us to watch! None of us know the length of our days on earth. Additionally, we know that many judgments will come upon the earth, and we know they will occur over a considerable period of time. Even before the great tribulation, we will see birth pangs consisting of wars, rumors of wars, famines and earthquakes in various places.

"You will hear of wars and rumors of wars, but see to it that you are not alarmed. Such things must happen, but the end is still to come. Nation will rise against nation, and kingdom against kingdom. There will be famines and earthquakes in various places. All these are the beginning of birth pains." (Matthew 24:6-8)

I have family and friends who travelled to the Philippines to provide help and assistance in the aftermath of typhoon Haiyan. This was one of the largest and most deadly typhoons in recorded history. They listened as the children told them that their families and friends, thousands of them, were literally lifted up and swept out to sea by this devastating storm. Unbelievably, just as in the days of Noah, *"the flood came and took them all away"* (see Matthew 24:37-39). Beloved, we are living in historic times! We never know the day or time when each of these catastrophic events will occur. In the aftermath of a great and tragic event, it may even seem that there is relative calm. However, we are warned in scripture to always be ready. We are warned that the birth pangs will increase in frequency and intensity. Even after the birth pangs, we will see the terrible apocalyptic events of the seals and the trumpets take place. All of these events will happen even before the bowls of wrath are finally poured out at the very end of the age.

As a whole, Jesus has already given us many, many warnings. He has also given us key events to watch for. He even assures us in very strong and sober words that His end time predictions will happen just like He says!

"Heaven and earth will pass away, but my words will never pass away." (Matthew 24:35)

The Manifold Wisdom and Great Mercy of the Maximized Harvest

It appears to me that Father God has established and ordered this whole end time scenario in such a way that it maximizes His harvest of souls. It appears that, in His great mercy, He has awaited the time that the largest number of souls in history are living on the earth. Then, after warning us for thousands and thousands of years about what will happen, He will begin, little by little, to pour out redemptive judgments on the earth in order to wake us up to turn back to Him and to receive His abundant grace. He knows that many of His own will not come to Him after each judgment. So, in His patience, He will do some shaking and bring in a harvest. Then He will wait a little bit longer. Then He will shake the earth and its inhabitants once again, this time a little harder, to bring in another harvest of souls. How merciful! He knows just how hard each of us need to be shaken before we will awaken. *But it is still up to us to respond.* How much shaking will it take for us to respond to Him and to join Him in His work in the vineyard?

We know that many will not respond or turn to Him. But, let us most certainly not be angry with those who join Him in His labors late in the day. How could we possibly be angry with Him because He is so generous? What it is that we deserved in the first place? We deserved death, but He gave us life! So, let us heartily and joyfully join Him in His labors to bring His life to others.

"Freely you have received; freely give." (Matthew 10:8)

Take note of what precedes that command: *"As you go, proclaim this message: 'The kingdom of heaven has come near.' Heal the sick, raise the dead, cleanse those who have leprosy, drive out demons." (Matthew 10:7-8)*

The greatest works will be required at the time of greatest need. Therefore, the fullest manifestation of Matthew 10:7-8 will come during the time of greatest need in world history. As His Holy fire pours out in greater and greater measure, the shaking will become harder and harder (see Revelation 8:1-5). As the shaking becomes harder and harder, our response, through Christ, will become more and more powerful. As a result, the harvest will increase exponentially!

The Parable of the Weeds

Jesus told them another parable: "The kingdom of heaven is like a man who sowed good seed in his field. But while everyone was sleeping, his enemy came and sowed weeds among the wheat, and went away. When the wheat sprouted and formed heads, then the weeds also appeared. The owner's servants came to him and said, 'Sir, didn't you sow good seed in your field? Where then did the weeds come from?' 'An enemy did this,' he replied. The servants asked him, 'Do you want us to go and pull them up?' 'No,' he answered, 'because while you are pulling the weeds, you may uproot the wheat with them. Let both grow together until the harvest. At that time I will tell the harvesters: First collect the weeds and tie them in bundles to be burned; then gather the wheat and bring it into my barn.'" (Matthew 13:28-30)

The Parable of the Weeds Explained

Then he left the crowd and went into the house. His disciples came to him and said, "Explain to us the parable of the weeds in the field." He answered, "The one who sowed the good seed is the Son of Man. The field is the world, and the good seed stands for the people of the kingdom. The weeds are the people of the evil one, and the enemy who sows them is the devil. The harvest is the end of the age, and the harvesters are angels. As the weeds are pulled up and burned in the fire, so it will be at the end of the age. The Son of Man will send out his angels, and they will weed out of his kingdom everything that causes sin and all who do evil. They will throw them into the blazing furnace, where there will be weeping and gnashing of teeth. Then the righteous will shine like the sun in the kingdom of their Father. Whoever has ears, let them hear." (Matthew 13:36-43)

Let us review the upcoming time of great restoration, merciful judgments and incredible harvest as revealed through the prophet Joel.

The Prophet Joel

"Do not be afraid, land of Judah; be glad and rejoice. Surely the Lord has done great things! Do not be afraid, you wild animals, for the pastures in the wilderness are becoming green. The trees are bearing their fruit; the fig tree and the vine yield their riches. Be glad, people of Zion, rejoice in the Lord your God, for he has given you the autumn rains because he is faithful. He sends you abundant showers, both autumn and spring rains, as before. The threshing floors will be filled with grain; the vats will overflow with new wine and oil. I will repay you for the years the locusts have eaten—the great locust and the young locust, the other locusts and the locust swarm—my great army that I sent among you. You will have plenty to eat, until you are full, and you will praise the name of the Lord your God, who has worked wonders for you; never again will my people be shamed. Then you will know that I am in Israel, that I am the Lord your God, and that there is no other; never again will my people be shamed."

The Day of the Lord

"And afterward, I will pour out my Spirit on all people. Your sons and daughters will prophesy, your old men will dream dreams, your young men will see visions. Even on my servants, both men and women, I will pour out my Spirit in those days. I will show wonders in the

heavens and on the earth, blood and fire and billows of smoke. The sun will be turned to darkness and the moon to blood before the coming of the great and dreadful day of the Lord. And everyone who calls on the name of the Lord will be saved; for on Mount Zion and in Jerusalem there will be deliverance, as the Lord has said, even among the survivors whom the Lord calls." (Joel 2:21-32)

5 | THE ROCK THAT CRUSHES

In c. 500 BC, the Babylonian king Nebuchadnezzar had an extraordinary and very detailed dream. It took the Lord, speaking through the prophet Daniel, to interpret it for him. In the dream, Nebuchadnezzar was shown kings and kingdoms that would rise and fall throughout history. But at the end, he was shown the ultimate Kingdom—the Kingdom of God. The dream concludes with the following.

> *While you were watching, a rock was cut out, but not by human hands. It struck the statue on its feet of iron and clay and smashed them. Then the iron, the clay, the bronze, the silver and the gold were all broken to pieces and became like chaff on a threshing floor in the summer. The wind swept them away without leaving a trace. But the rock that struck the statue became a huge mountain and filled the whole earth. (Daniel 2:34-35)*

> *In the time of those kings, the God of heaven will set up a kingdom that will never be destroyed, nor will it be left to another people. It will crush all those kingdoms and*

bring them to an end, but it will itself endure forever. This is the meaning of the vision of the rock cut out of a mountain, but not by human hands—a rock that broke the iron, the bronze, the clay, the silver and the gold to pieces. The great God has shown the king what will take place in the future. The dream is true and its interpretation is trustworthy. (Daniel 2:44-45)

Who is the rock not cut by human hands? Who is the rock that crushes all the other kingdoms? The answer comes from the "Rock" himself. Two verses where Jesus gives the answer to this question are Matthew 21:44 and 22:44.

In the first of those two verses, Jesus is talking to the chief priests and Pharisees. The Creator and King of the universe—the God of pure, righteous love—was standing right in front of them in human form, but they didn't recognize Him. They didn't recognize Him because they didn't know God. They didn't *have* Love abiding in their hearts. In fact, they were challenging and rejecting Him. Jesus told them, *"Anyone who falls on this stone will be broken to pieces; anyone on whom it falls will be crushed"* (Matthew 21:44). He was identifying Himself as the Rock eternal—the *"Rock that Crushes."*

Later, in Matthew 22:44, Jesus was again talking to the Pharisees. He told them that King David was writing about Jesus when he penned Psalm 110 (there is a wealth of revelation about Jesus in Psalm 110). But at the end of the chapter, we read the following, *"The Lord is at your right hand; he will crush kings on the day of his wrath. He will judge the nations, heaping up the dead and crushing the rulers of the whole earth. He will drink from a brook along the way, and so he will lift his head high"* (Psalm 110:5-7).

What should we glean from this? We know that Jesus Christ is patient, kind, humble and long-suffering. He is a

Servant. He is Love. Love is the essence of His nature. He was first crushed for us, dying on the cross; and He has been long-suffering in waiting for us to come to repentance. He is the Christ. He is the Messiah. He is the Anointed One. He is the King of the whole earth. He is the King of the entire universe. He holds everything together. However, we must remember that the time of choosing—the valley of decision—will come to a close. This is true for each of us, as well as for all of humanity. Anyone that is not with Him (with Love) is against Him (against Love), and will ultimately be crushed and destroyed. It does not matter how influential or powerful that a person is right now. All of the demonically empowered worldly kings and kingdoms that join the Oppressor in oppressing mankind must fall! Jesus Christ will take them down; and He will do it alongside His faithful followers. Jesus Christ will rule and reign with His beloved ones!

For some of us, at least in the western world, looking around today from our current state of relative comfort and freedom, this whole concept of Jesus as a "Rock that Crushes" may seem a little extreme. However, consider, for example, North Korea. North Korea is today a terrible persecutor and oppressor of Christians. North Korea is typically considered the number one persecutor of Christians in the modern world, out of about 60 countries where a significant level of persecution of Christians takes place today. North Korea has established a government-sponsored religion that everyone must obey under the threat of imprisonment, torture and even death. Everyone is required to have certain images (pictures) of the ruling family ancestors hung on their wall in a particular way. Those who disobey are put into prison indefinitely. If the government finds a Bible in a home? The response is again the threat of indefinite imprisonment and torture, often eventually leading to death.

Right next door to North Korea is arguably the most powerful missionary-sending and praying nation in the world—South Korea. What if these two countries were a type or shadow of what we may someday see across most of the earth? What if we saw a large confederation of nations that came together and acted much like North Korea is acting today? What if they established a government-sponsored religion that everyone must obey under threat of banishment, punishment or even death? I think under those circumstances we would better understand what it means to cry out to the Lord for justice. I believe we would possess a heart cry for His "Kingdom of Love" to be established on the earth and for the evil oppressing rulers to be overcome by our righteous King! In those circumstances, Psalm 110 might even become part of our prayers: *"The Lord is at your right hand; he will crush kings on the day of his wrath. He will judge the nations, heaping up the dead and crushing the rulers of the whole earth."*

Today, are you standing on the Rock Eternal? Is your foundation built on Him? Remember that, *"In the time of those kings, the God of heaven will set up a kingdom that will never be destroyed, nor will it be left to another people. It will crush all those kingdoms and bring them to an end, but it will itself endure forever"* (Daniel 2:44).

Do you want to be a part of His Kingdom of Love? Let me just take a moment to ask you a very critical question. Have you given your whole life to Jesus Christ? If you are reading this, it means that you are still alive. Therefore, you have been given at least one more breath, one more gracious moment to choose what is right, one more moment to choose Love—to choose Life! In this moment, let us all fall on the Rock by yielding ourselves to the King and asking that His burning, passionate love would completely fill our hearts, burning out anything that would oppose Him! Then, let us join with Him to accomplish His goal of destroying the works of Satan and bringing His Kingdom of Love to the earth. On earth as it is in heaven. Amen!

6 | BEHOLD THE BEAUTY, THE GOODNESS AND THE SEVERITY OF THE LORD

Therefore consider the goodness and severity of God: on those who fell, severity; but toward you, goodness, if you continue in His goodness. Otherwise you also will be cut off. (Romans 11:22, NKJV)

As long as we have breath in our lungs, and as long as we have a heartbeat, we are still being shown great mercy and grace by the Lord. We are also living in a period of grace within history. But each of us have our own personal period of grace—the gift of our living days on earth. His mercies are new every morning and His love never ceases (see Lamentation 3:22-23). Each day is given to us as a precious gift. Each day is another opportunity to turn to our loving Father and receive the great love He is offering each one of us, to return that love to Him and to freely give it to others. Each day is another opportunity to gratefully serve the One who created us, formed us and sustains us with our every breath and every one of our heartbeats. God is love. Love is who He is. Love is what He does. Love is His everlasting posture and position. Whether or not we will believe that He truly loves us, and then actually receive His love, that may be another story—that is up to us!

Let us consider a parable. Let's say that a man, whom the Lord dearly loves, was out enjoying the day, driving his convertible out in the sunshine with the top down. He was driving down the road with happiness in his heart, singing along to the music on the radio. Up ahead, unbeknownst to this man, a bridge was out. The bridge typically extended over a very high crevasse. So, the man was actually driving on a path that seemed enjoyable, but was leading to destruction.

Let's say that the Lord, knowing the situation, sent a mighty eagle. The eagle flew down and attacked the man. The attack caused the man to get some scratches and resulted in considerable pain. But, due to the eagle attack, the man pulled his car over to the side of the road, avoiding certain death.

Would this divine act of God be considered wrath, judgment or mercy? The man could have decided that God is a mean and vindictive Father. Why else would he send an eagle to scratch him up and cause him pain, ruining an otherwise beautiful and enjoyable day?! The man might have chosen to curse God and also the eagle, and then to drive off down the road again.

On the other hand, the man might have decided to take a moment to consider what just happened. Perhaps he could haven taken some time to get his bearings and to see his true circumstances. He might have then discovered the cliff and the fact that the bridge was out, proceeding to turn around and drive the other way, giving the thanks and praise to the Lord that He rightly deserves!

In our journey with the Lord, we must always remember that our understanding of reality is relatively small and insignificant compared to that of our God and Maker. Only God can see the end from the beginning!

> *Let the wicked forsake their ways and the unrighteous their thoughts. Let them turn to the Lord, and he will have mercy on them, and to our God, for he will freely pardon. "For my thoughts are not your thoughts, neither are your ways my ways," declares the Lord. "As the heavens are higher than the earth, so are my ways higher than your ways and my thoughts than your thoughts." (Isaiah 55:7-9)*

We must learn to trust and obey Father God at all times. When something that appears negative or painful happens, we must learn to take a breath, get our bearings and ask the Father for wisdom and guidance.

Consider also if a man or woman were in sound, peaceful sleep. However, unbeknownst to them, they risked sleeping through and missing out on something wonderful that would change their lives forever. Perhaps a friend who knew about this wonderful thing came and discovered them sleeping and attempted to awaken them. But, even when the friend spoke to them, they did not even stir. What if they didn't even awaken to shouting? Should their friend have just given up at that point and walked away? Would it be considered rude to shake them or prod them to get them to wake up, only to receive the wonderful thing that they had always desired? If they had a negative reaction or experienced shock when they were seemingly rudely awakened, wouldn't it be short-lived? Their gratefulness, however, would last forever!

We must remember that if we would not stray from the Lord, or become dull or apathetic, we would not have to be shaken. Wouldn't it be true to say that the further we have strayed from the Lord, the harder He may have to shake us to wake us? Furthermore, if He did shake us to wake us, wouldn't that be mercy and grace? If we were on a path to destruction and God let us continue without waking us, wouldn't He be exhibiting indifference or contempt? What if we missed out on something that was most lovely, beautiful, wondrous and eternal because He left us sleeping? Would that be the action of a loving Father? Since we don't have a complete picture of what is going on in our lives, we must seek wisdom from the Father always.

There is a time coming when good and evil will mature to their fullest measures. During that time, those perpetuating evil will experience their fullest measures of shaking, which is in essence, mercy and grace from the Lord. The shaking will continue until the time of grace has ended, both for individuals and also for everyone on the earth. Those who are asleep will have their final warnings to wake up and turn to the Lord. Scores of people will turn to the Lord during this great and final harvest! Yet, others will decide against Him and oppose Him. Some will even choose to fight Him in battle! The decision to oppose Him is regretful to our Savior, since the Lord wishes that all would come to repentance (see 2 Peter 3:9). Those that oppose Him will eventually run out of merciful judgments and will enter into His wrath.

Enter into the rock, and hide in the dust, from the terror of the Lord and the glory of His majesty. The lofty looks of man shall be humbled, the haughtiness of men shall be bowed down, and the Lord alone shall be exalted in that day. For the day of the Lord of hosts shall come upon everything proud and lofty, upon everything lifted up— and it shall be brought low—upon all the cedars of Lebanon that are high and lifted up, and upon all the oaks of Bashan; upon all the high mountains, and upon all the hills that are lifted up; upon every high tower, and upon every fortified wall; upon all the ships of Tarshish, and upon all the beautiful sloops. The loftiness of man shall be bowed down, and the haughtiness of men shall be brought low; the Lord alone will be exalted in that day, but the idols He shall utterly abolish. They shall go into the holes of the rocks, and into the caves of the earth, from the terror of the Lord and the glory of His majesty, when He arises to shake the earth mightily. (Isaiah 2:10-21, NKJV)

"Surely the eyes of the Sovereign Lord are on the sinful kingdom. I will destroy it from the face of the earth. Yet I will not totally destroy the descendants of Jacob," declares the Lord. "For I will give the command, and I will shake the people of Israel among all the nations as grain is shaken in a sieve, and not a pebble will reach the ground. All the sinners among my people will die by the sword, all those who say, 'Disaster will not overtake or meet us.'

Israel's Restoration

"In that day I will restore David's fallen shelter—I will repair its broken walls and restore its ruins—and will rebuild it as it used to be, so that they may possess the remnant of Edom and all the nations that bear my name," declares the Lord, who will do these things. "The days are coming," declares the Lord, "when the reaper will be overtaken by the plowman and the planter by the one treading grapes. New wine will drip from the mountains and flow from all the hills, and I will bring my people Israel back from exile. "They will rebuild the ruined cities and live in them. They will plant vineyards and drink their wine; they will make gardens and eat

their fruit. I will plant Israel in their own land, never again to be uprooted from the land I have given them," says the Lord your God. (Amos 9:8-15)

7 | THE ARMY OF THE LIGHT (PERFECT LOVE CASTS OUT FEAR)

Perfected in Love

There are two vital things that the Spirit of Truth has been showing me in recent months. First, He has been showing me that Jesus loves us more than we think He does. Secondly, He has been showing me that Father God's plans for us are better than we think they are. Despite the fact that these two things are Biblical truths, we often struggle to comprehend them. They require the revelation of the Holy Spirit.

The Holy Spirit may reveal things to us in many different ways. For example, when the Holy Spirit shows us something, we may later find it, or seemingly stumble upon it, in the Bible. It is His Word. It is already firmly established in the heavens. *"Your word, Lord, is eternal; it stands firm in the heavens"* (Psalm 119:89). We should always be asking Him and seeking for Him to reveal to us some more of that firmly established Word. If we know what the Father is saying and doing, we will then know what to say and do.

*"Ask and it will be given to you; seek and you will find;
knock and the door will be opened to you. For everyone
who asks receives; he who seeks finds; and to him who
knocks, the door will be opened." (Matthew 7:7-8)*

In our regular daily Bible study, the Lord may highlight a
Bible verse and then shed light on it by the power of the Holy
Spirit. Or He may give us a specific Bible verse reference to
look up in order to provide a unique word for that particular
time or season. Or He may speak a word to us and then
provide a Bible verse to go along with it. Or He may have
someone else speak a word directly to us that we just
"happen" to later find in the Bible. There are many, many
ways He can speak to us. However, all of these avenues
require the Holy Spirit to reveal His words to us. Otherwise
we will just have words without power, life or meaning.
*(Note: I always recommend inviting the Holy Spirit, the Spirit
of Truth, to help in your regular Bible study times. Remember
that the Holy Spirit is also called the "Helper," see John 14:26).*

As the Lord was speaking to my spirit about the fact that
He loves us more than we think He does, I began to share
that word with others. Several weeks later, I ran across a
somewhat familiar Bible scripture that actually explained it.
It was in a prayer of the apostle Paul for the Ephesians.

*...that He would grant you, according to the riches of His
glory, to be strengthened with power through His Spirit
in the inner man, so that Christ may dwell in your hearts
through faith; and that you, being rooted and grounded
in love, may be able to comprehend with all the saints
what is the breadth and length and height and depth,
and to know the love of Christ which surpasses
knowledge, that you may be filled up to all the fullness of
God. (Ephesians 3:16-19, NASB)*

70

We need to be aware of, and freely receive, *"the love of Christ which surpasses knowledge."* We need to know that Jesus Christ loves us more than we think, more than our ability to understand. We will continue to receive new and increasing revelation of His love for all of eternity. We must have faith to believe He (Love) exists. We must believe Him in order to receive Him. Once we believe Him and freely receive Him, we can then fulfill the law and the prophets by returning His love back to Him (with all of our mind, soul and strength) and by freely giving Him (Love) to others, whom like us, also don't deserve Him.

"Freely you received, freely give."(Matthew 10:8)

Jesus replied: "'Love the Lord your God with all your heart and with all your soul and with all your mind.' This is the first and greatest commandment. And the second is like it: 'Love your neighbor as yourself.' All the Law and the Prophets hang on these two commandments."
(Matthew 22:37-40)

And without faith it is impossible to please God, because anyone who comes to him must believe that he exists and that he rewards those who earnestly seek him.
(Hebrews 11:6)

Our most kind, merciful and loving Father has great plans for us in His eternal Kingdom of Love.

"For I know the plans I have for you," declares the Lord, "plans to prosper you and not to harm you, plans to give you hope and a future." (Jeremiah 29:11)

"What no eye has seen, what no ear has heard, and what

no human mind has conceived"—the things God has prepared for those who love him—these are the things God has revealed to us by his Spirit. The Spirit searches all things, even the deep things of God. (I Corinthians 2:9-10)

But what are the details of His amazing plan? Once again, we must always remember to ask Him.

"Then you will call on me and come and pray to me, and I will listen to you. You will seek me and find me when you seek me with all of your heart." (Jeremiah 29:12-13)

"Call to me and I will answer you and tell you great and unsearchable things you do not know." (Jeremiah 33:3)

Once we being to understand and receive the extravagant love of Christ, our fears begin to vacate and are replaced by His love, joy and peace.

God is love. Whoever lives in love lives in God, and God in him. In this way, love is made complete among us so that we will have confidence on that day of judgment, because in this world we are like Him. There is no fear in love. But perfect love drives out fear, because fear has to do with punishment. The one who fears is not made perfect in love. We love because He first loves us. (I John 4:16-19)

What does perfect love look like? Jesus explains this in Matthew 5 and Luke 6.

"If you love those who love you, what credit is that to you? Even sinners love those who love them. And if you

do good to those who are good to you, what credit is that to you? Even sinners do that. And if you lend to those from whom you expect repayment, what credit is that to you? Even sinners lend to sinners, expecting to be repaid in full. But love your enemies, do good to them, and lend to them without expecting to get anything back. Then your reward will be great, and you will be children of the Most High, because he is kind to the ungrateful and wicked. Be merciful, just as your Father is merciful." (Luke 6:32-36)

We may ask, "Do you mean that we have to love even the really bad people? Even people that hatefully oppose us?" Jesus said, *"...I tell you, love your enemies and pray for those who persecute you, that you may be children of your Father in heaven"* (Matthew 5:44).

This leads us right back to Jesus' command in Matthew 10:8, *"Freely you received, freely give."* Once we receive this love freely (without having earned it, or having deserved it), we must also give it freely to others that haven't earned it or deserved it. This sets us free from having to figure out if someone deserves our love and attention or not. First of all, no, they don't deserve it, and neither did we! Nobody does! Secondly, it is the Father's love, and He commands us to give it away! The love did not come from us in the first place. It came from above. We have no right to withhold it!

Once we begin to live according to this revelation, we being to grow up and begin to look more like our Abba Father in heaven. We will then also begin to understand and live out Jesus' command when He said, *"Be perfect, therefore, as your heavenly Father is perfect"* (Matthew 5:48).

Living and abiding in this kind of love is the only way that we can *"overcome evil with good"* (Romans 12:21).

Perfected in Fearlessness

We must come to understand that to be perfected in love is also to be perfected in fearlessness. It is only the love and joy of Jesus Christ that will make us fearless enough to die for Him. It is the love of Christ that will cause us to, *"not love [our] lives so much as to shrink from death"* as we overcome the devil, who uses fear as a weapon of battle and destruction (see Revelation 12:11).

> *"Who shall separate us from the love of Christ? Shall trouble or hardship or persecution or famine or nakedness or danger or sword? As it is written: 'For your sake we face death all day long; we are considered sheep to be slaughtered.' No, in all these things we are more than conquerors through Him who loved us. For I am convinced that neither death nor life, neither angels nor demons, neither the present nor the future, nor any powers, neither height nor depth, nor anything else in all creation, will be able to separate us from the love of God that is in Christ Jesus our Lord." (Romans 8:35-39)*

In these increasingly dark days, let us be completely filled with the love of the Father and with the Holy Spirit and fire! Let the love of Christ consume us so completely that it burns out all fear, compromise and any sin. Let us become a burning bush, a light for all to see as the glory of the Lord rests upon us; let many be drawn to the light and may we lead many people to their Bridegroom and King!

The Glory of Zion

"Arise, shine, for your light has come, and the glory of the Lord rises upon you. See, darkness covers the earth

and thick darkness is over the peoples, but the Lord rises upon you and his glory appears over you. Nations will come to your light, and kings to the brightness of your dawn. Lift up your eyes and look about you: All assemble and come to you; your sons come from afar, and your daughters are carried on the hip. Then you will look and be radiant, your heart will throb and swell with joy; the wealth on the seas will be brought to you, to you the riches of the nations will come." (Isaiah 60:1-5)

It is time for the fearless warriors of the King to arise, go up and take His land! Remember, Jesus said He would always be with us, even to the end of the age.

"Be strong and courageous. Do not be afraid or terrified because of them, for the Lord your God goes with you; he will never leave you nor forsake you." (Deuteronomy 31:6)

Whoever dwells in the shelter of the Most High will rest in the shadow of the Almighty. I will say of the Lord, "He is my refuge and my fortress, my God, in whom I trust." Surely he will save you from the fowler's snare and from the deadly pestilence. He will cover you with his feathers, and under his wings you will find refuge; his faithfulness will be your shield and rampart. You will not fear the terror of night, nor the arrow that flies by day, nor the pestilence that stalks in the darkness, nor the plague that destroys at midday. A thousand may fall at your side, ten thousand at your right hand, but it will not come near you. You will only observe with your eyes and see the punishment of the wicked. If you say, 'The Lord is my refuge' and you make the Most High your dwelling, no harm will overtake you, no disaster will come near your tent. For he will command his angels concerning you to guard you in all your ways; they will lift you up in their hands, so that you will not strike your foot against a stone. You will tread on the lion and the cobra; you will trample the great lion and the serpent. "Because he loves me," says the Lord, "I will rescue him; I will protect him, for he acknowledges my name. He will call on me, and I will answer him; I will be with him in trouble, I will deliver him and honor him. With long life I will satisfy him and show him my salvation." (Psalm 91)

Because you have guarded and kept My word of patient endurance [have held fast the lesson of My patience with the expectant endurance that I give you], I also will keep you [safe] from the hour of trial (testing) which is coming on the whole world to try those who dwell upon the earth. (Revelation 3:10, AMP)

But, how will God keep us from the hour of trial, testing, disaster and plague? Just like He did for Moses and the Israelites—supernaturally!

The fifth angel sounded his trumpet, and I saw a star that had fallen from the sky to the earth. The star was given the key to the shaft of the Abyss. When he opened the Abyss, smoke rose from it like the smoke from a gigantic furnace. The sun and sky were darkened by the smoke from the Abyss. And out of the smoke locusts came down on the earth and were given power like that of scorpions of the earth. They were told not to harm the grass of the earth or any plant or tree, but only those people who did not have the seal of God on their foreheads. (Revelation 9:1-4)

For in the day of trouble he will keep me safe in his dwelling; he will hide me in the shelter of his sacred tent and set me high upon a rock. Then my head will be exalted above the enemies who surround me; at his sacred tent I will sacrifice with shouts of joy; I will sing and make music to the Lord. (Psalm 27:5-6)

8 | LABORING IN THE HARVEST

Throughout the Bible we find the theme of seedtime and harvest. We know from the Scriptures that the final harvest of good and evil will happen at the end of the age. Let's explore what the Spirit of God is saying to us regarding our role in this great harvest.

Boaz is seen as a type of Christ in the Bible. Let us begin by watching closely what is happening as we see Boaz returning to the *"field"* (which represents the *"world"* in Matthew 13).

Naomi said to her, "Go ahead, my daughter." So she [Ruth] went out, entered a field and began to glean behind the harvesters. As it turned out, she was working in a field belonging to Boaz, who was from the clan of Elimelek. Just then Boaz arrived from Bethlehem and greeted the harvesters, "The Lord be with you!" "The Lord bless you!" they answered. (Ruth 2:2-4)

What did Boaz find his people doing when he returned? They were busy bringing in the harvest! They were joyfully doing as they were expected, just as they had been earlier instructed. They were accomplishing these assignments while anticipating his return.

Remember that when Jesus was in Jerusalem, He said,

"For I tell you, you will not see me again until you say, 'Blessed is he who comes in the name of the Lord.'" *(Matthew 23:39)*

God does not change His mind. When He says something, He means it! There is no crooked word that comes out of His mouth. So, what are our instructions? What should He find us doing when He returns? I think it is clear that in addition to watching and praying, we should be bringing His Kingdom of Love to earth! We should be actively demonstrating and sharing His love with others and bringing in His harvest; we should be reaping for Him the rewards of His suffering.

"My food," said Jesus, "is to do the will of him who sent me and to finish his work. Don't you have a saying, 'It's still four months until harvest'? I tell you, open your eyes and look at the fields! They are ripe for harvest. Even now the one who reaps draws a wage and harvests a crop for eternal life, so that the sower and the reaper may be glad together. Thus the saying 'One sows and another reaps' is true. I sent you to reap what you have not worked for. Others have done the hard work, and you have reaped the benefits of their labor." (John 4:34-38)

It takes a fearless warrior, operating in the love of Christ, to bring in an abundant harvest. Evil must be overcome with good. When our enemy is overcome, we can then release the prisoners and set them free!

"If your enemy is hungry, feed him; if he is thirsty, give him something to drink. In doing this, you will heap burning coals on his head." Do not be overcome by evil, but overcome evil with good. (Romans 12:20-21)

"In fact, no one can enter a strong man's house without

first tying him up. Then he can plunder the strong man's house." (Mark 3:27)

The Spirit of the Sovereign Lord is on me, because the Lord has anointed me to proclaim good news to the poor. He has sent me to bind up the brokenhearted, to proclaim freedom for the captives and release from darkness for the prisoners, to proclaim the year of the Lord's favor and the day of vengeance of our God, to comfort all who mourn, and provide for those who grieve in Zion—to bestow on them a crown of beauty instead of ashes, the oil of joy instead of mourning, and a garment of praise instead of a spirit of despair. They will be called oaks of righteousness, a planting of the Lord for the display of his splendor. (Isaiah 61:1-3)

As followers of Jesus Christ, what will we do? Will we respond to His commands? Or will we sit around in ignorance, apathy and cowardice, waiting for Him to return? Consider the parable of the talents. How did the Master respond to the one who hid in a hole and waited for the Master's return, instead of laboring in his Master's harvest? Let us consider the actions of the wicked servant in the Parable of the Talents.

"Then the man who had received one bag of gold came. 'Master,' he said, 'I knew that you are a hard man, harvesting where you have not sown and gathering where you have not scattered seed. So I was afraid and went out and hid your gold in the ground. See, here is what belongs to you.' His master replied, 'You wicked, lazy servant! So you knew that I harvest where I have not sown and gather where I have not scattered seed? Well then, you should have put my money on deposit with the bankers, so that when I returned I would have received it back with interest. So take the bag of gold from him and give it to the one who has ten bags. For whoever has will be given more, and they will have an

abundance. Whoever does not have, even what they have will be taken from them. And throw that worthless servant outside, into the darkness, where there will be weeping and gnashing of teeth."' (Matthew 25:24-30)

Consider how the wicked servant said, *"I was afraid and went out and hid your gold..."* Notice how similar that is to what Adam said after he had sinned and turned his authority over to Satan. *"I heard you in the garden, and I was afraid because I was naked; so I hid"* (see Genesis 3:10).

Christ has already won the victory and holds all authority. So, let us never go down the road of holding back or hiding again! Instead, let us faithfully and courageously lay down our lives for our brothers and sisters around us and around the world, just as Christ did for us! Let it then be said to us on that day, *"Well done, good and faithful servant! You have been faithful with a few things; I will put you in charge of many things. Come and share your master's happiness!"* (Matthew 25:21).

Then Jesus came to them and said, "All authority in heaven and on earth has been given to me. Therefore go and make disciples of all nations, baptizing them in the name of the Father and of the Son and of the Holy Spirit, and teaching them to obey everything I have commanded you. And surely I am with you always, to the very end of the age." (Matthew 28:18-20)

"As you go, proclaim this message: 'The kingdom of heaven has come near.' Heal the sick, raise the dead, cleanse those who have leprosy, drive out demons. Freely you have received; freely give." (Matthew 10:7-8)

"But the cowardly, the unbelieving, the vile, the murderers, the sexually immoral, those who practice magic arts, the idolaters and all liars—they will be consigned to the fiery lake of burning sulfur. This is the second death." (Revelation 21:8)

Those who are wise will shine like the brightness of the heavens, and those who lead many to righteousness, like the stars for ever and ever. (Daniel 12:3)

9 | WARRING IN THE SPIRIT: PRAYER, FASTING AND WORSHIP

Our Heavenly Father has established prayer, fasting and worship as integral elements of His end time plan. Let us start by exploring how our Lord will use prayer and fasting at end of the age.

Prayer and Fasting

Let us take note in the Scriptures how day and night prayer is tied to Christ's return.

> *For Zion's sake I will not keep silent, for Jerusalem's sake I will not remain quiet, till her vindication shines out like the dawn, her salvation like a blazing torch. The nations will see your vindication, and all kings your glory; you will be called by a new name that the mouth of the Lord will bestow. You will be a crown of splendor in the Lord's hand, a royal diadem in the hand of your God. No longer will they call you Deserted, or name your land Desolate. But you will be called Hephzibah, and your land Beulah;*

for the Lord will take delight in you, and your land will be married. As a young man marries a young woman, so will your Builder marry you; as a bridegroom rejoices over his bride, so will your God rejoice over you. I have posted watchmen on your walls, Jerusalem; they will never be silent day or night. You who call on the Lord, give yourselves no rest, and give him no rest till he establishes Jerusalem and makes her the praise of the earth. (Isaiah 62:1-7)

Then Jesus told his disciples a parable to show them that they should always pray and not give up...

"...will not God bring about justice for his chosen ones, who cry out to him day and night? Will he keep putting them off? I tell you, he will see that they get justice, and quickly. However, when the Son of Man comes, will he find faith on the earth?" (Luke 18:1,7-8)

Notice that when Jesus returns again to the earth and to Jerusalem, it is in response to the saints who are crying out day and night in prayer. Even King David cried out, *"Rise up, O God, judge the earth, for all the nations are your inheritance"* (Psalm 82:8).

In the book of Revelation, we see again how the prayers of the saints are used by God to enact His purposes on the earth at the opening of the seventh seal and the beginning the trumpet judgments, which ultimately end with the announcement of Jesus coming to set up His Kingdom on the earth.

When he opened the seventh seal, there was silence in heaven for about half an hour. And I saw the seven angels who stand before God, and seven trumpets were given to them. Another angel, who had a golden censer, came and stood at the altar. He was given much incense to offer, with the prayers of all God's people, on the golden altar in front of the throne. The smoke of the incense, together with the prayers of God's people, went up before God from the angel's hand. Then the angel took the censer, filled it with fire from the altar, and hurled it on the earth; and there came peals of thunder, rumblings, flashes of lightning and an earthquake. (Revelation 8:1-5)

When Jesus walked this earth, He alluded to the fact that we would fast for His return after He left.

"How can the guests of the bridegroom fast while he is with them? They cannot, so long as they have him with them. But the time will come when the bridegroom will be taken from them, and on that day they will fast." (Mark 2:19-20)

The prophet Joel declared in prophecy a fast in the face of great calamity, at the great and terrible Day of the Lord.

The day of the Lord is great; it is dreadful. Who can endure it? "Even now," declares the Lord, "return to me with all your heart, with fasting and weeping and mourning." Rend your heart and not your garments. Return to the Lord your God, for he is gracious and compassionate, slow to anger and abounding in love, and he relents from sending calamity. Who knows? He may turn and relent and leave behind a blessing—grain offerings and drink offerings for the Lord your God. Blow the trumpet in Zion, declare a holy fast, call a sacred assembly. Gather the people, consecrate the assembly;

bring together the elders, gather the children, those nursing at the breast. Let the bridegroom leave his room and the bride her chamber. Let the priests, who minister before the Lord, weep between the portico and the altar. Let them say, "Spare your people, Lord. Do not make your inheritance an object of scorn, a byword among the nations. Why should they say among the peoples, 'Where is their God?'" (Joel 2:11-17)

Consider also the words of the prophet Zephaniah concerning the great Day of the Lord.

Gather together, gather yourselves together, you shameful nation, before the decree takes effect and that day passes like windblown chaff, before the Lord's fierce anger comes upon you, before the day of the Lord's wrath comes upon you. Seek the Lord, all you humble of the land, you who do what he commands. Seek righteousness, seek humility; perhaps you will be sheltered on the day of the Lord's anger. (Zephaniah 2:1-3)

The prophet Amos also saw the great Day coming.

"In that day," declares the Sovereign Lord, "I will make the sun go down at noon and darken the earth in broad daylight. I will turn your religious festivals into mourning and all your singing into weeping. I will make all of you wear sackcloth and shave your heads. I will make that time like mourning for an only son and the end of it like a bitter day." (Amos 8:9-10)

The prophet Zechariah tells of that great Day. That Day will come when many nations surround Jerusalem to besiege the city once again. On that Day the people will cry out to Jesus in prayer; they will be weeping and travailing for His return.

"And I will pour out on the house of David and the inhabitants of Jerusalem a spirit of grace and supplication. They will look on me, the one they have pierced, and they will mourn for him as one mourns for an only child, and grieve bitterly for him as one grieves for a firstborn son. On that day the weeping in Jerusalem will be as great as the weeping of Hadad Rimmon in the plain of Megiddo. The land will mourn, each clan by itself, with their wives by themselves: the clan of the house of David and their wives, the clan of the house of Nathan and their wives, the clan of the house of Levi and their wives, the clan of Shimei and their wives, and all the rest of the clans and their wives. On that day a fountain will be opened to the house of David and the inhabitants of Jerusalem, to cleanse them from sin and impurity." (Zechariah 12:10-14,13:1)

And as we see in Isaiah 62 and Luke 18, when His people cry out to Him, He will answer!

Warfare Worship

You have taught children and infants to tell of your strength [to give you praise], silencing your enemies and all who oppose you. (Psalm 8:2, NLT)

Worship and warfare are intertwined throughout the Holy Scriptures. Consider, for example, David's Song of Praise.

He said: "The Lord is my rock, my fortress and my deliverer; my God is my rock, in whom I take refuge, my shield and the horn of my salvation. He is my stronghold, my refuge and my savior—from violent people you save me. I called to the Lord, who is worthy of praise, and have been saved from my enemies. The waves of death swirled about me; the torrents of destruction overwhelmed me. The cords of the grave coiled around me; the snares of death confronted me. In my distress I called to the Lord; I called out to my God. From his temple he heard my voice; my cry came to his ears. The earth trembled and quaked, the foundations of the heavens shook; they trembled because he was angry. Smoke rose from his nostrils; consuming fire came from his mouth, burning coals blazed out of it. He parted the heavens and came down; dark clouds were under his feet. He mounted the cherubim and flew; he soared on the wings of the wind. He made darkness his canopy around him—the dark rain clouds of the sky. Out of the brightness of his presence bolts of lightning blazed forth. The Lord thundered from heaven; the voice of the Most High resounded. He shot his arrows and scattered the enemy, with great bolts of lightning he routed them. The valleys of the sea were exposed and the foundations of the earth laid bare at the rebuke of the Lord, at the blast of breath from his nostrils. He reached down from on high and took hold of me; he drew me out of deep waters. He rescued me from my powerful enemy, from my foes, who were too strong for me. They confronted me in the day of my disaster, but the Lord was my support. He brought me out into a spacious place; he rescued me because he delighted in me." (2 Samuel 22:2-20)

Throughout history, we have often seen the Lord instructing His people to advance against their enemies with trumpets, with shouts of proclamation, and with songs of worship and praise.

Then the Lord said to Joshua, "See, I have delivered Jericho into your hands, along with its king and its fighting men. March around the city once with all the armed men. Do this for six days. Have seven priests carry trumpets of rams' horns in front of the ark. On the seventh day, march around the city seven times, with the priests blowing the trumpets. When you hear them sound a long blast on the trumpets, have the whole army give a loud shout; then the wall of the city will collapse and the army will go up, everyone straight in." (Joshua 6:2-5)

Gideon and the hundred men with him reached the edge of the camp at the beginning of the middle watch, just after they had changed the guard. They blew their trumpets and broke the jars that were in their hands. The three companies blew the trumpets and smashed the jars. Grasping the torches in their left hands and holding in their right hands the trumpets they were to blow, they shouted, "A sword for the Lord and for Gideon!" While each man held his position around the camp, all the Midianites ran, crying out as they fled. When the three hundred trumpets sounded, the Lord caused the men throughout the camp to turn on each other with their swords. (Judges 7:19-22)

"You will not have to fight this battle. Take up your positions; stand firm and see the deliverance the Lord will give you, Judah and Jerusalem. Do not be afraid; do

not be discouraged. Go out to face them tomorrow, and the Lord will be with you..."

"...Listen to me, Judah and people of Jerusalem! Have faith in the Lord your God and you will be upheld; have faith in his prophets and you will be successful." After consulting the people, Jehoshaphat appointed men to sing to the Lord and to praise him for the splendor of his holiness as they went out at the head of the army, saying: "Give thanks to the Lord, for his love endures forever." As they began to sing and praise, the Lord set ambushes against the men of Ammon and Moab and Mount Seir who were invading Judah, and they were defeated. (2 Chronicles 20:17, 20-22)

Every stroke the Lord lays on them with his punishing club will be to the music of timbrels and harps, as he fights them in battle with the blows of his arm. (Isaiah 30:32)

The theme of warfare worship continues throughout the New Testament.

About midnight Paul and Silas were praying and singing hymns to God, and the other prisoners were listening to them. Suddenly there was such a violent earthquake that the foundations of the prison were shaken. At once all the prison doors flew open, and everyone's chains came loose. (Acts 16:25-26)

It seems that Paul and Silas were taking Jesus at His word when they said, *"rejoice and be glad,"* even when you are facing your enemy, even when you are persecuted (see Matthew 5). How is this possible? I believe that this is done simply out of faith and in obedience to the Lord. However, we know that the joy of the Lord is our strength.

I have not personally been through very much persecution compared to the apostles and many other believers throughout the world today. Yet, I can also surmise from what I have heard and read from persecuted believers, that there is a supernatural supply of the oil of the joy of the Lord that comes with persecution. For example, I remember hearing several months ago of Steve (Steve is a pseudonym used for security reasons). Steve is a ministry leader who was caught in the Middle East and was tortured by electrocution by the authorities of the country he was laboring in. When he was interviewed, he was described as being "filled with the joy of the Lord," as he explained how his bones still ached; yet, he was "proud" of the Lord for keeping him alive! Another amazing believer who suffered persecution recently reported that he lamented missing the joy of the Lord that came during his times of suffering. Perhaps we can see in these stories the "fellowship of Christ's sufferings," mentioned by the apostle Paul (see Philippians 3:10).

As we approach the end of the age, we reach the fullness of times. It should be no surprise that the Kingdom of God on the earth is proclaimed with a trumpet, with a shout and with worship! The greatest manifestation of warfare worship will come forth at the end of this age—at the beginning of the reign of Jesus Christ as King on the earth!

"Immediately after the distress of those days 'the sun will be darkened, and the moon will not give its light; the stars will fall from the sky, and the heavenly bodies will be shaken.' Then will appear the sign of the Son of Man in heaven. And then all the peoples of the earth will mourn when they see the Son of Man coming on the

clouds of heaven, with power and great glory. And he will send his angels with a loud trumpet call, and they will gather his elect from the four winds, from one end of the heavens to the other." (Matthew 24:29-31)

The seventh angel sounded his trumpet, and there were loud voices in heaven, which said: "The kingdom of the world has become the kingdom of our Lord and of his Messiah, and he will reign for ever and ever." And the twenty-four elders, who were seated on their thrones before God, fell on their faces and worshiped God, saying: "We give thanks to you, Lord God Almighty, the One who is and who was, because you have taken your great power and have begun to reign. The nations were angry, and your wrath has come. The time has come for judging the dead, and for rewarding your servants the prophets and your people who revere your name, both great and small—and for destroying those who destroy the earth." Then God's temple in heaven was opened, and within his temple was seen the ark of his covenant. And there came flashes of lightning, rumblings, peals of thunder, an earthquake and a severe hailstorm. (Revelation 11:15-19)

Threefold Hallelujah Over Babylon's Fall

After this I heard what sounded like the roar of a great multitude in heaven shouting:

"Hallelujah! Salvation and glory and power belong to our God, for true and just are his judgments. He has condemned the great prostitute who corrupted the earth by her adulteries. He has avenged on her the blood of his servants."

And again they shouted:

"Hallelujah! The smoke from her goes up for ever and ever."

The twenty-four elders and the four living creatures fell down and worshiped God, who was seated on the throne.

And they cried:

"Amen, Hallelujah!"
Then a voice came from the throne, saying:

"Praise our God, all you his servants, you who fear him, both great and small!"

Then I heard what sounded like a great multitude, like the roar of rushing waters and like loud peals of thunder, shouting:

"Hallelujah! For our Lord God Almighty reigns. Let us rejoice and be glad and give him glory! For the wedding of the Lamb has come, and his bride has made herself ready. Fine linen, bright and clean, was given her to wear." (Fine linen stands for the righteous acts of God's holy people.) (Revelation 19:1-8)

Sing to the Lord a new song, his praise in the assembly of his faithful people. Let Israel rejoice in their Maker; let the people of Zion be glad in their King. Let them praise his name with dancing and make music to him with timbrel and harp. For the Lord takes delight in his people; he crowns the humble with victory. Let his faithful people rejoice in this honor and sing for joy on their beds. May the praise of God be in their mouths and a double-edged sword in their hands, to inflict vengeance on the nations and punishment on the peoples, to bind their kings with fetters, their nobles with shackles of iron, to carry out the sentence written against them—this is the glory of all his faithful people. Praise the Lord. (Psalm 149:1-7)

We see another remarkable depiction of this worship scene in Isaiah 24. First, we see a terrifying description of the destruction of the whole earth at the end of the age. It seems as if the devastation is complete and that there is practically no one left. But suddenly we see something beautiful and wondrous arising on the earth.

The Lord's Devastation of the Earth

See, the Lord is going to lay waste the earth and devastate it; he will ruin its face and scatter its inhabitants—it will be the same for priest as for people, for the master as for his servant, for the mistress as for her servant, for seller as for buyer, for borrower as for lender, for debtor as for creditor. The earth will be completely laid waste and totally plundered. The Lord has spoken this word. The earth dries up and withers, the world languishes and withers, the heavens languish with the earth. The earth is defiled by its people; they have disobeyed the laws, violated the statutes and broken the everlasting covenant. Therefore a curse consumes the earth; its people must bear their guilt. Therefore earth's inhabitants are burned up, and very few are left...

...They raise their voices, they shout for joy; from the west they acclaim the Lord's majesty. Therefore in the east give glory to the Lord'; exalt the name of the Lord, the God of Israel, in the islands of the sea. From the ends of the earth we hear singing: 'Glory to the Righteous One.' (Isaiah 24:1-6, 14-16)

As the scene continues to unfold, the Lord returns with great glory—even unto the embarrassment of the sun and moon—to reign in Jerusalem on Mount Zion! We see an even more descriptive illustration of this global worship scene unveiling in Psalm 98 and 99.

Sing to the Lord a new song, for he has done marvelous things; his right hand and his holy arm have worked salvation for him [See also Isaiah 63]. The Lord has made his salvation known and revealed his righteousness to the nations. He has remembered his love and his faithfulness to Israel; all the ends of the earth have seen the salvation of our God. Shout for joy to the Lord, all the earth, burst into jubilant song with music; make music to the Lord with the harp, with the harp and the sound of singing, with trumpets and the blast of the ram's horn—shout for joy before the Lord, the King. Let the sea resound, and everything in it, the world, and all who live in it. Let the rivers clap their hands, let the mountains sing together for joy; let them sing before the Lord, for he comes to judge the earth. He will judge the world in righteousness and the peoples with equity. The Lord reigns, let the nations tremble; he sits enthroned between the cherubim, let the earth shake. Great is the Lord in Zion; he is exalted over all the nations. Let them praise your great and awesome name—he is holy. (Psalm 98, 99:1-3)

Can we have worship and joy in the midst of great tumult? Yes! Why is that? Because that is what heaven is like! I don't believe what goes on around the Throne of God is boring. It is an awesome, powerful and noisy place! The enemy cannot stand against it! When Ezekiel saw it, it literally floored him! Part of what he saw was a great commotion.

When the creatures moved, I heard the sound of their wings, like the roar of rushing waters, like the voice of the Almighty, like the tumult of an army. (Ezekiel 1:24)

We must remember that when we worship our Lord, we are worshipping a Great and Mighty Warrior!

The Lord is a warrior; the Lord is his name. (Exodus 15:3)

I saw heaven standing open and there before me was a white horse, whose rider is called Faithful and True. With justice he judges and wages war. His eyes are like blazing fire, and on his head are many crowns. He has a name written on him that no one knows but he himself. He is dressed in a robe dipped in blood, and his name is the Word of God. The armies of heaven were following him, riding on white horses and dressed in fine linen, white and clean. Coming out of his mouth is a sharp sword with which to strike down the nations. 'He will rule them with an iron scepter.' He treads the winepress of the fury of the wrath of God Almighty. On his robe and on his thigh he has this name written: KING OF KINGS AND LORD OF LORDS. (Revelation 19:11-16)

Let this be written for a future generation, that a people not yet created may praise the Lord: "The Lord looked down from his sanctuary on high, from heaven he viewed the earth, to hear the groans of the prisoners and release those condemned to death." So the name of the Lord will be declared in Zion and his praise in Jerusalem when the peoples and the kingdoms assemble to worship the Lord. (Psalm 102:18-22)

10 | WARRING IN THE SPIRIT: PERSECUTION AND MARTYRDOM

Has the Lord Jesus ever spoken to you regarding the possibility of persecution, or even volunteering to give up your life as a martyr for Him and His Kingdom? This is a very important topic for us to consider, especially in respect to the times we are now entering. Persecution and martyrdom are at the forefront of prophetic scripture dealing with the end times.

The Shedding of Blood: Persecution and Martyrdom

Jesus laid down His life for His Bride. He was mocked, ridiculed, rejected, beaten and killed to make a way for us.

He was despised and rejected by mankind, a man of suffering, and familiar with pain. Like one from whom people hide their faces he was despised, and we held him in low esteem. (Isaiah 53:3)

All who see me mock me; they hurl insults, shaking their

heads. *"He trusts in the Lord,"* they say, *"let the Lord rescue him. Let him deliver him, since he delights in him." (Psalm 22:7-8)*

What does He expect of us in return? Jesus said,

"Whoever wants to be my disciple must deny themselves and take up their cross and follow me." (Matthew 16:24)

Jesus also said,

"Blessed are those who are persecuted because of righteousness, for theirs is the kingdom of heaven. Blessed are you when people insult you, persecute you and falsely say all kinds of evil against you because of me. Rejoice and be glad, because great is your reward in heaven, for in the same way they persecuted the prophets who were before you." (Matthew 5:10-12)

"Remember what I told you: 'A servant is not greater than his master.' If they persecuted me, they will persecute you also." (John 15:20)

The apostle Paul gave us further insight into the reality of suffering persecution for our Lord Jesus Christ.

In fact, everyone who wants to live a godly life in Christ Jesus will be persecuted... (2 Timothy 3:12)

To this very hour we go hungry and thirsty, we are in rags, we are brutally treated, we are homeless. We work hard with our own hands. When we are cursed, we bless; when we are persecuted, we endure it; when we are slandered, we answer kindly. We have become the scum of the earth, the garbage of the world—right up to this moment. (I Corinthians 4:11-13)

I want to know Christ—yes, to know the power of his resurrection and participation in his sufferings, becoming like him in his death, and so, somehow, attaining to the resurrection from the dead. (Philippians 3:10-11)

Historical accounts tell us that eleven out of the twelve disciples were martyred. It is also recorded that enemies attempted to kill John the apostle, but that he wouldn't die.

Although it may be hard to accurately enumerate, it is estimated that from when Jesus walked the earth until now, there have been as many as 70 million Christian martyrs. Some believe that 40 million of those martyrs came forth in the 20th century alone! The number of martyrs for Christ that we see now every year may be among the highest in history.

What about us? Persecution is one thing. But will we again risk the same fate as the disciples did in their day? How many of us will actually face martyrdom? Let us consider the scriptures concerning this subject.

As Jesus was sitting on the Mount of Olives, the disciples came to him privately. 'Tell us," they said, "when will this happen, and what will be the sign of your coming and of the end of the age?" Jesus answered: "Watch out that no one deceives you. For many will come in my name, claiming, 'I am the Messiah,' and will deceive many. You will hear of wars and rumors of wars, but see to it that you are not alarmed. Such things must happen, but the end is still to come. Nation will rise against nation, and kingdom against kingdom. There will be famines and earthquakes in various places. All these are the beginning of birth pains. Then you will be handed over to be persecuted and put to death, and you will be hated by all nations because of me. At that time many will turn away from the faith and will betray and hate each other, and many false prophets will appear and deceive many people. Because of the increase of wickedness, the love of most will grow cold, but the one who stands firm to the end will be saved." (Matthew 24:3-13)

"The ten horns are ten kings who will come from this kingdom. After them another king will arise, different from the earlier ones; he will subdue three kings. He will speak against the Most High and oppress his holy people and try to change the set times and the laws. The holy people will be delivered into his hands for a time, times and half a time. 'But the court will sit, and his power will be taken away and completely destroyed forever. Then the sovereignty, power and greatness of all the kingdoms under heaven will be handed over to the holy people of the Most High. His kingdom will be an everlasting kingdom, and all rulers will worship and obey him.'" (Daniel 7:24-27)

"His armed forces will rise up to desecrate the temple fortress and will abolish the daily sacrifice. Then they will set up the abomination that causes desolation. With flattery he will corrupt those who have violated the covenant, but the people who know their God will firmly resist him. Those who are wise will instruct many, though for a time they will fall by the sword or be burned or captured or plundered. When they fall, they will receive a little help, and many who are not sincere

will join them. Some of the wise will stumble, so that they may be refined, purified and made spotless until the time of the end, for it will still come at the appointed time." *(Daniel 11:31-35)*

The man clothed in linen, who was above the waters of the river, lifted his right hand and his left hand toward heaven, and I heard him swear by him who lives forever, saying, "It will be for a time, times and half a time. When the power of the holy people has been finally broken, all these things will be completed." (Daniel 12:7)

"So when you see standing in the holy place 'the abomination that causes desolation,' spoken of through the prophet Daniel—let the reader understand—then let those who are in Judea flee to the mountains. Let no one on the housetop go down to take anything out of the house. Let no one in the field go back to get their cloak. How dreadful it will be in those days for pregnant women and nursing mothers! Pray that your flight will not take place in winter or on the Sabbath. For then there will be great distress, unequaled from the beginning of the world until now—and never to be equaled again. If those days had not been cut short, no one would survive, but for the sake of the elect those days will be shortened. At that time if anyone says to you, 'Look, here is the Messiah!' or, 'There he is!' do not believe it. For false messiahs and false prophets will appear and perform great signs and wonders to deceive, if possible, even the elect. See, I have told you ahead of time. So if anyone tells you, 'There he is, out in the wilderness,' do not go out; or, 'Here he is, in the inner rooms,' do not believe it. For as lightning that comes from the east is visible even in the west, so will be the

coming of the Son of Man. Wherever there is a carcass, there the vultures will gather.

> *"Immediately after the distress of those days*

> *"'the sun will be darkened, and the moon will not give its light; the stars will fall from the sky, and the heavenly bodies will be shaken.'*

"Then will appear the sign of the Son of Man in heaven. And then all the peoples of the earth will mourn when they see the Son of Man coming on the clouds of heaven, with power and great glory. And he will send his angels with a loud trumpet call, and they will gather his elect from the four winds, from one end of the heavens to the other." (Matthew 24:15-31)

The woman was given the two wings of a great eagle, so that she might fly to the place prepared for her in the wilderness, where she would be taken care of for a time, times and half a time, out of the serpent's reach. Then from his mouth the serpent spewed water like a river, to overtake the woman and sweep her away with the torrent. But the earth helped the woman by opening its mouth and swallowing the river that the dragon had spewed out of his mouth. Then the dragon was enraged at the woman and went off to wage war against the rest of her offspring—those who keep God's commands and hold fast their testimony about Jesus. (Revelation 12:14-17)

Do not be afraid of what you are about to suffer. I tell you, the devil will put some of you in prison to test you, and you will suffer persecution for ten days. Be faithful, even to the point of death, and I will give you life as your victor's crown. Whoever has ears, let them hear what the

Spirit says to the churches. The one who is victorious will not be hurt at all by the second death. (Revelation 2:10)

When he opened the fifth seal, I saw under the altar the souls of those who had been slain because of the word of God and the testimony they had maintained. They called out in a loud voice, 'How long, Sovereign Lord, holy and true, until you judge the inhabitants of the earth and avenge our blood?' Then each of them was given a white robe, and they were told to wait a little longer, until the full number of their fellow servants, their brothers and sisters, were killed just as they had been. (Revelation 9:6-11)

The beast was given a mouth to utter proud words and blasphemies and to exercise its authority for forty-two months. It opened its mouth to blaspheme God, and to slander his name and his dwelling place and those who live in heaven. It was given power to wage war against God's holy people and to conquer them. And it was given authority over every tribe, people, language and nation. All inhabitants of the earth will worship the beast—all whose names have not been written in the Lamb's book of life, the Lamb who was slain from the creation of the world. Whoever has ears, let them hear. "If anyone is to go into captivity, into captivity they will go. If anyone is to be killed with the sword, with the sword they will be killed." This calls for patient endurance and faithfulness on the part of God's people. (Revelation 13:5-10)

A third angel followed them and said in a loud voice: "If anyone worships the beast and its image and receives its mark on their forehead or on their hand, they, too, will drink the wine of God's fury, which has been poured full strength into the cup of his wrath. They will be tormented with burning sulfur in the presence of the holy angels and of the Lamb. And the smoke of their torment will rise for ever and ever. There will be no rest day or night for those who worship the beast and its image, or for anyone who receives the mark of its name." This calls for patient endurance on the part of the people of God who keep his commands and remain faithful to Jesus. Then I heard a voice from heaven say, "Write this: Blessed are the dead who die in the Lord from now on." "Yes," says the Spirit, "they will rest from their labor, for their deeds will follow them." (Revelation 14:9-13)

After this I looked, and there before me was a great multitude that no one could count, from every nation, tribe, people and language, standing before the throne and before the Lamb. They were wearing white robes and were holding palm branches in their hands...

...Then one of the elders asked me, 'These in white robes—who are they, and where did they come from?' I answered, "Sir, you know." And he said, "These are they who have come out of the great tribulation; they have washed their robes and made them white in the blood of the Lamb. Therefore, they are before the throne of God and serve him day and night in his temple; and he who sits on the throne will shelter them with his presence. 'Never again will they hunger; never again will they thirst.'" (Revelation 7:9,13-16)

They triumphed over him [Satan] by the blood of the Lamb and by the word of their testimony; they did not love their lives so much as to shrink from death. (Revelation 12:11)

106

I saw thrones on which were seated those who had been given authority to judge. And I saw the souls of those who had been beheaded because of their testimony about Jesus and because of the word of God. They had not worshiped the beast or its image and had not received its mark on their foreheads or their hands. They came to life and reigned with Christ a thousand years. (The rest of the dead did not come to life until the thousand years were ended.) This is the first resurrection. Blessed and holy are those who share in the first resurrection. The second death has no power over them, but they will be priests of God and of Christ and will reign with him for a thousand years. (Revelation 20:4-6)

As persecution of the followers of Jesus Christ increases across the earth right through the end of the age, what should our response be? Let us be encouraged that the blood of our persecution and suffering is adding seed to the end time harvest and will play a significant role in ushering in the Kingdom of God on the earth. Let us look now to the Word of God.

And they sang a new song, saying: "You are worthy to take the scroll and to open its seals, because you were slain, and with your blood you purchased for God persons from every tribe and language and people and nation." (Revelation 5:9)

"As long as the earth endures, seedtime and harvest, cold and heat, summer and winter, day and night will never cease." (Genesis 8:22)

Be joyful in hope, patient in affliction, faithful in prayer.

Share with the Lord's people who are in need. Practice hospitality. Bless those who persecute you; bless and do not curse. Rejoice with those who rejoice; mourn with those who mourn. Live in harmony with one another. Do not be proud, but be willing to associate with people of low position. Do not be conceited. Do not repay anyone evil for evil. Be careful to do what is right in the eyes of everyone. If it is possible, as far as it depends on you, live at peace with everyone. Do not take revenge, my dear friends, but leave room for God's wrath, for it is written: "It is mine to avenge; I will repay," says the Lord. On the contrary: "If your enemy is hungry, feed him; if he is thirsty, give him something to drink. In doing this, you will heap burning coals on his head." Do not be overcome by evil, but overcome evil with good. (Romans 12:12-21)

Remember those earlier days after you had received the light, when you endured in a great conflict full of suffering. Sometimes you were publicly exposed to insult and persecution; at other times you stood side by side with those who were so treated. You suffered along with those in prison and joyfully accepted the confiscation of your property, because you knew that you yourselves had better and lasting possessions. So do not throw away your confidence; it will be richly rewarded. You need to persevere so that when you have done the will of God, you will receive what he has promised. For,

> *"In just a little while, he who is coming will come and will not delay."*

And,

> *"But my righteous one will live by faith. And I take*

no pleasure in the one who shrinks back."

But we do not belong to those who shrink back and are destroyed, but to those who have faith and are saved. (Hebrews 10:32-39)

More Than Conquerors

What, then, shall we say in response to these things? If God is for us, who can be against us? He who did not spare his own Son, but gave him up for us all—how will he not also, along with him, graciously give us all things? Who will bring any charge against those whom God has chosen? It is God who justifies. Who then is the one who condemns? No one. Christ Jesus who died—more than that, who was raised to life—is at the right hand of God and is also interceding for us. Who shall separate us from the love of Christ? Shall trouble or hardship or persecution or famine or nakedness or danger or sword? As it is written:

> *"For your sake we face death all day long; we are considered as sheep to be slaughtered."*

No, in all these things we are more than conquerors through him who loved us. For I am convinced that neither death nor life, neither angels nor demons, neither the present nor the future, nor any powers, neither height nor depth, nor anything else in all creation, will be able to separate us from the love of God that is in Christ Jesus our Lord. (Romans 8:31-39)

We are Always at War—Until We Win

We must remember that at all times we are at open war. We have been born into this conflict. Our enemy will not take a break until we take Him out. Therefore, we must always remember to put on our full armor and take the fight to our adversary, the devil. We must meet him readily in battle. This is a serious war. We must faithfully persevere, endure and not grow weary in well doing. Beloved, we are in it to win it! We must never give up, even at the risk of death.

For though we walk (live) in the flesh, we are not carrying on our warfare according to the flesh and using mere human weapons. For the weapons of our warfare are not physical [weapons of flesh and blood], but they are mighty before God for the overthrow and destruction of strongholds, [Inasmuch as we] refute arguments and theories and reasonings and every proud and lofty thing that sets itself up against the [true] knowledge of God; and we lead every thought and purpose away captive into the obedience of Christ (the Messiah, the Anointed One), Being in readiness to punish every [insubordinate for his] disobedience, when your own submission and obedience [as a church] are fully secured and complete. (I Corinthians 10:3-6, AMP)

Put on God's whole armor [the armor of a heavy-armed soldier which God supplies], that you may be able successfully to stand up against [all] the strategies and the deceits of the devil. For we are not wrestling with flesh and blood [contending only with physical opponents], but against the despotisms, against the powers, against [the master spirits who are] the world rulers of this present darkness, against the spirit forces of wickedness in the heavenly (supernatural) sphere. Therefore put on God's complete armor, that you may be able to resist and stand your ground on the evil day [of danger], and, having done all [the crisis demands], to stand [firmly in your place]. Stand therefore [hold your ground], having tightened the belt of truth around your loins and having put on the breastplate of integrity and of moral rectitude and right standing with God, And having shod your feet in preparation [to face the enemy with the firm-footed stability, the promptness, and the readiness produced by the good news] of the Gospel of peace. Lift up over all the [covering] shield of saving faith, upon which you can quench all the flaming missiles of the wicked [one]. And take the helmet of salvation and the sword that the Spirit wields, which is the Word of God. Pray at all times (on every occasion, in every season) in the Spirit, with all [manner of] prayer and entreaty. To that end keep alert and watch with strong purpose and perseverance, interceding in behalf of all the saints (God's consecrated people). (Ephesians 6:11-18, AMP)

But you, keep your head in all situations, endure hardship, do the work of an evangelist, discharge all the duties of your ministry. For I am already being poured out like a drink offering, and the time for my departure is near. I have fought the good fight, I have finished the race, I have kept the faith. Now there is in store for me the crown of righteousness, which the Lord, the righteous Judge, will award to me on that day—and not only to me, but also to all who have longed for his appearing. (2 Timothy 4:5-8)

11 | SIGNS AND WONDERS—THE GREATER WORKS

Jesus said, *"Very truly I tell you, whoever believes in me will do the works I have been doing, and they will do even greater things than these, because I am going to the Father"* (John 14:12). Let us dive further into the subject of the greater works.

We know from the Word that in a time of great darkness, there will be great light. We find this throughout the whole Bible. The wheat and the tares mature together (see Matthew 13). The darkness and the light will continue to build up and increase, and they will not stop increasing until the end of the age. They will increase even through the last three and one-half years of this age, just prior to the return of Christ! We find evidence of this in the book of Daniel.

> *"And forces shall be mustered by him, and they shall defile the sanctuary fortress; then they shall take away the daily sacrifices, and place there the abomination of desolation. Those who do wickedly against the covenant he shall corrupt with flattery; but the people who know*

their God shall be strong, and carry out great exploits. And those of the people who understand shall instruct many; yet for many days they shall fall by sword and flame, by captivity and plundering." (Daniel 11:31-33, NKJV)

During the period of time Jesus said will be the most difficult the world will ever see (see Matthew 24:21-22), what do we find the saints doing? What are the fully mature wheat accomplishing on the earth? They are carrying out great exploits, instructing new believers and leading many souls to Jesus Christ—even in the face of the greatest time of adversity!

The theme of great light in deep darkness is not new to us. We see it prophesied well before Jesus ever appeared on the earth.

The people walking in darkness have seen a great light; on those living in the land of deep darkness a light has dawned. You have enlarged the nation and increased their joy; they rejoice before you as people rejoice at the harvest, as warriors rejoice when dividing the plunder. For as in the day of Midian's defeat, you have shattered the yoke that burdens them, the bar across their shoulders, the rod of their oppressor. Every warrior's boot used in battle and every garment rolled in blood will be destined for burning, will be fuel for the fire. For to us a child is born, to us a son is given, and the government will be on his shoulders. And he will be called Wonderful Counselor, Mighty God, Everlasting Father, Prince of Peace. Of the greatness of his government and peace there will be no end. He will reign on David's throne and over his kingdom, establishing and upholding it with justice and righteousness from that time on and forever. The zeal of the Lord Almighty will accomplish this. (Isaiah 9:2-7)

Somebody might say, "Well, Jesus is the light of the world." That is true. But He came so that He could live in and through us! When He lives in us, we *"have the light of life."* So we should not be surprised that Jesus went on to describe us in the same way. Let us consider the words of Jesus and the prophet Isaiah.

"I am the light of the world. Whoever follows me will never walk in darkness, but will have the light of life." (John 8:12)

"As long as it is day, we must do the works of him who sent me. Night is coming, when no one can work. While I am in the world, I am the light of the world." (John 9:4-5)

"You are the light of the world. A town built on a hill cannot be hidden. Neither do people light a lamp and put it under a bowl. Instead they put it on its stand, and it gives light to everyone in the house. In the same way, let your light shine before others, that they may see your good deeds and glorify your Father in heaven." (Matthew 5:14-16)

We cannot abdicate our role and responsibility to shine during the dark and difficult times. We are to joyfully embrace the light and be the light to the world!

"Arise, shine, for your light has come, and the glory of the Lord rises upon you. See, darkness covers the earth and thick darkness is over the peoples, but the Lord rises upon you and his glory appears over you. Nations will

come to your light, and kings to the brightness of your dawn. 'Lift up your eyes and look about you: All assemble and come to you; your sons come from afar, and your daughters are carried on the hip. Then you will look and be radiant, your heart will throb and swell with joy; the wealth on the seas will be brought to you, to you the riches of the nations will come." (Isaiah 60:1-5)

The Lord is looking for burning ones who will blaze brightly in dark times. The Psalmist said, *"You, Lord, keep my lamp burning; my God turns my darkness into light"* (Psalm 18:28). Jesus said, *"Be dressed ready for service and keep your lamps burning, like servants waiting for their master to return from a wedding banquet, so that when he comes and knocks they can immediately open the door for him"* (Luke 12:35-36).

When we are on fire with the love of Christ, we become a curious sight to those in deep darkness, just like the burning bush was a curious sight to Moses. When our hearts are on fire with the Holy Spirit, His Holy fire will be burning in our eyes, it will be radiating from our countenance, it will be coming out of our hands and it will be proceeding out of our mouths!

For the Son of Man in his day will be like the lightning, which flashes and lights up the sky from one end to the other. (Luke 17:24)

God came from Teman, the Holy One from Mount Paran. His glory covered the heavens and his praise filled the earth. His splendor was like the sunrise; rays flashed from his hand, where his power was hidden. (Habakkuk 3:3-4)

Sun and moon stood still in the heavens at the glint of

your flying arrows, at the lightning of your flashing spear. In wrath you strode through the earth and in anger you threshed the nations. You came out to deliver your people, to save your anointed one. (Habakkuk 3:11-13)

"Out of the brightness of his presence bolts of lightning blazed forth. The Lord thundered from heaven; the voice of the Most High resounded. He shot his arrows and scattered the enemy, with great bolts of lightning he routed them. The valleys of the sea were exposed and the foundations of the earth laid bare at the rebuke of the Lord, at the blast of breath from his nostrils. He reached down from on high and took hold of me; he drew me out of deep waters. He rescued me from my powerful enemy, from my foes, who were too strong for me. They confronted me in the day of my disaster, but the Lord was my support. He brought me out into a spacious place; he rescued me because he delighted in me." (2 Samuel 22:10-20)

I looked up and there before me was a man dressed in linen, with a belt of fine gold from Uphaz around his waist. His body was like topaz, his face like lightning, his eyes like flaming torches, his arms and legs like the gleam of burnished bronze, and his voice like the sound of a multitude. (Daniel 10:5-7)

The hair on his head was white like wool, as white as snow, and his eyes were like blazing fire. (Revelation 1:14)

His face was like the sun shining in all its brilliance. (Revelation 1:16)

I want to be more like Jesus, don't you? We must press on to Jesus, just as when Moses approached the mountain of the Lord. We must yield our hearts to Him and let Him set our hearts on fire, before His Holy fire will emanate from our eyes, mouths, face and hands.

Then Moses said to him, "If your Presence does not go with us, do not send us up from here. How will anyone know that you are pleased with me and with your people unless you go with us? What else will distinguish me and your people from all the other people on the face of the earth?" And the Lord said to Moses, "I will do the very thing you have asked, because I am pleased with you and I know you by name." Then Moses said, "Now show me your glory. (Exodus 33:15-18)

When Aaron and all the Israelites saw Moses, his face was radiant, and they were afraid to come near him. (Exodus 34:30)

Place me like a seal over your heart, like a seal on your arm; for love is as strong as death, its jealousy unyielding as the grave. It burns like blazing fire, like a mighty flame. Many waters cannot quench love; rivers cannot sweep it away. (Song of Songs 8:6-7)

"Your eye is the lamp of your body. When your eyes are healthy, your whole body also is full of light. But when they are unhealthy, your body also is full of darkness. See to it, then, that the light within you is not darkness. Therefore, if your whole body is full of light, and no part of it dark, it will be just as full of light as when a lamp shines its light on you." (Luke 11:33-36)

"A good man brings good things out of the good stored up in his heart, and an evil man brings evil things out of the evil stored up in his heart. For the mouth speaks what the heart is full of." (Luke 6:45)

But if I say, "I will not mention his word or speak anymore in his name," his word is in my heart like a fire, a fire shut up in my bones. I am weary of holding it in; indeed, I cannot. (Jeremiah 20:9)

When the fire of the Holy Spirit comes up from our hearts and proceeds out our mouths, the Kingdom of God is built up and established, while the wisdom of the world and demonic strongholds are uprooted and destroyed.

Therefore this is what the Lord God Almighty says: "Because the people have spoken these words, I will make my words in your mouth a fire and these people the wood it consumes." (Jeremiah 5:14)

Therefore have I hewn down and smitten them by means of the prophets; I have slain them by the words of My mouth; My judgments [pronounced upon them by you prophets] are like the light that goes forth. (Hosea 6:5, AMP)

For the weapons of our warfare are not physical [weapons of flesh and blood], but they are mighty before God for the overthrow and destruction of strongholds, [Inasmuch as we] refute arguments and theories and reasonings and every proud and lofty thing that sets itself up against the [true] knowledge of God... (2 Corinthians 10:4-5, AMP)

My message and my preaching were not with wise and persuasive words, but with a demonstration of the Spirit's power, so that your faith might not rest on human wisdom, but on God's power. We do, however, speak a message of wisdom among the mature, but not the wisdom of this age or of the rulers of this age, who are coming to nothing. No, we declare God's wisdom, a mystery that has been hidden and that God destined for our glory before time began. None of the rulers of this age understood it, for if they had, they would not have crucified the Lord of glory. (I Corinthians 2:4-8)

"You must be on your guard. You will be handed over to the local councils and flogged in the synagogues. On account of me you will stand before governors and kings as witnesses to them. And the gospel must first be preached to all nations. Whenever you are arrested and brought to trial, do not worry beforehand about what to say. Just say whatever is given you at the time, for it is not you speaking, but the Holy Spirit." (Mark 13:9-11)

I show you specified new things from this time forth, even hidden things [kept in reserve] which you have not known. They are created now [called into being by the prophetic word], and not long ago; and before today you have never heard of them, lest you should say, Behold, I knew them! (Isaiah 48:6-7, AMP)

In the end times, the *"demonstration of the Spirit's power"* through the spoken word will take on new dimensions that we would currently find difficult to comprehend (see I Corinthians 2:4-8). This is like what the Lord spoke of through the prophet Habakkuk.

Look around [you, Habakkuk, replied the Lord] among the nations and see! And be astonished! Astounded! For I am putting into effect a work in your days [such] that you would not believe it if it were told you. (Habakkuk 1:5, AMP)

The wisdom of this world will crumble, as Jesus' glorious light and His Holy fire are spread across the earth.

The Lord says: "These people come near to me with their mouth and honor me with their lips, but their hearts are far from me. Their worship of me is based on merely human rules they have been taught. Therefore once more I will astound these people with wonder upon wonder; the wisdom of the wise will perish, the intelligence of the intelligent will vanish." (Isaiah 29:13-14)

"And I will appoint my two witnesses, and they will prophesy for 1,260 days, clothed in sackcloth." They are "the two olive trees" and the two lampstands, and "they stand before the Lord of the earth." If anyone tries to harm them, fire comes from their mouths and devours their enemies. This is how anyone who wants to harm them must die. They have power to shut up the heavens so that it will not rain during the time they are prophesying; and they have power to turn the waters into blood and to strike the earth with every kind of plague as often as they want. (Revelation 11:3-6)

In many of the previous passages of scripture, one can clearly see the Holy fire proceeding from the Father, Jesus, the two witnesses, Moses and the prophets. Are we to just sit back and wait for Jesus, a prophet, or an angel to speak and accomplish these great and mighty works on their own? Have you ever considered that He might be waiting for you to ask Him to fill you with His Holy fire, so He can flow in and through you?

When Moses approached the Red Sea, it appears in scripture that Moses was standing there waiting on God to do His thing. But we see later that God was also waiting on Moses. God wanted to work with and through Moses. God didn't want Moses and the Israelites to stand there in fear, staring at the Red Sea on one side and the Egyptians coming from the other side. He needed Moses and the Israelites to step up in faith and do their part!

> *Then the Lord said to Moses, "Why are you crying out to me? Tell the Israelites to move on. Raise your staff and stretch out your hand over the sea to divide the water so that the Israelites can go through the sea on dry ground. I will harden the hearts of the Egyptians so that they will go in after them. And I will gain glory through Pharaoh and all his army, through his chariots and his horsemen." (Exodus 14:15-17)*

I get the sense from this exchange that God was saying, *"Ok, Moses, I've given you authority and you know my heart. You see the enemy coming for you and the Red Sea is in front of you. So, what are you going to do about it?"*

What about us? He's filled us with His precious Holy Spirit. He's given us the authority to trample on snakes and scorpions and all forms of evil (see Luke 10:19). Are we going to respond by hiding, or by just standing there and staring in fear and terror at the giants in front of us—at the gross sin and the disasters on the earth? Instead, aren't we ready to step up, step out and be a Holy Spirit fire pyro for

Jesus? I believe that Jesus and all of His creation are waiting for us! They're waiting for all of us to come forth and make our move! Jesus said, *"I have come to bring fire on the earth, and how I wish it were already kindled!"* (Luke 12:49).

> *For I consider that the sufferings of this present time are not worthy to be compared with the glory which shall be revealed in us. For the earnest expectation of the creation eagerly waits for the revealing of the sons of God. For the creation was subjected to futility, not willingly, but because of Him who subjected it in hope; because the creation itself also will be delivered from the bondage of corruption into the glorious liberty of the children of God. (Romans 8:18-21, NKJV)*

Should not the sons of God be about doing what the Son and His Father are doing? Shouldn't we follow Christ's example of radiating light and love—bringing the Kingdom of Heaven to earth? Let us review again Isaiah 61.

> *The Spirit of the Sovereign Lord is on me, because the Lord has anointed me to proclaim good news to the poor. He has sent me to bind up the brokenhearted, to proclaim freedom for the captives and release from darkness for the prisoners, to proclaim the year of the Lord's favor and the day of vengeance of our God, to comfort all who mourn, and provide for those who grieve in Zion—to bestow on them a crown of beauty instead of ashes, the oil of joy [see Psalm 45:7] instead of mourning, and a garment of praise instead of a spirit of despair. They will be called oaks of righteousness, a planting of the Lord for the display of his splendor. They will rebuild the ancient ruins and restore the places long devastated; they will renew the ruined cities that have*

been devastated for generations. Strangers will shepherd your flocks; foreigners will work your fields and vineyards. And you will be called priests of the Lord, you will be named ministers of our God. You will feed on the wealth of nations, and in their riches you will boast. Instead of your shame you will receive a double portion, and instead of disgrace you will rejoice in your inheritance. And so you will inherit a double portion in your land, and everlasting joy will be yours. (Isaiah 61:1-7)

Let us not wait for the two witnesses to come forth and testify for us. I believe the two witnesses will come forth in the end times. I believe they are most likely Elijah and Moses; I believe they may also symbolize the Christians and the Messianic Jews. However, we do know for certain from the commands of Jesus that it is our job to disciple the nations and boldly speak forth the gospel of the Kingdom.

"But you will receive power when the Holy Spirit comes on you; and you will be my witnesses in Jerusalem, and in all Judea and Samaria, and to the ends of the earth." (Acts 1:8)

And this gospel of the kingdom will be preached in the whole world as a testimony to all nations, and then the end will come. (Matthew 24:14)

It should not surprise us that the greatest works in history will come at the time of greatest need. Have you ever noticed in the Bible that there is a lot of spiritual darkness, devastation, death and destruction during the end of the age? During the birth pangs, the seals and the trumpets, for example, there are plagues, sicknesses, diseases and demons being released. There are people dying from war and from all kinds of natural disasters. But, what is more powerful: Life or Death? Love or Hate? We all know that answer. And we must live it during this time! This will be an amazing time for the love, power and Holy fire of Christ to flow through us to bring an answer to all of these terrible things that are going on across the earth. When we bring the answer, we will lead multitudes to Christ. But let's not wait for the very last few years to do this. Let us jump in the river and start now!

Once again, at the end of the age we will witness the fullest manifestation of the following scripture.

> *"As you go, proclaim this message: 'The kingdom of heaven has come near.' Heal the sick, raise the dead, cleanse those who have leprosy, drive out demons. Freely you have received; freely give." (Matthew 10:7-8)*

Our faithfulness and obedience during this time will lead to great reward.

> *Those who are wise will shine like the brightness of the heavens, and those who lead many to righteousness, like the stars for ever and ever. (Daniel 12:3)*

12 | THE FINAL CONFLICT

As we begin to consider the final conflict between good and evil at the end of the age, we may find it difficult to imagine. We know from the book of Revelation that the conflict takes place during the final phase of the great tribulation—the seven bowls of wrath (see Revelation 15-19). In this final conflict, we see Jesus battling alongside the saints, riding on a white horse with a double-edged sword coming out of His mouth! How will this battle actually unfold? Will *all* of the saints actively participate in the battle? How will they actually engage in it? I have many questions about the details of this conflict. However, the Bible gives us a substantial amount of information regarding this battle. It paints a very interesting *and very graphic* picture. I think we'd be best served to ask the Holy Spirit for revelation as we study the scriptures pertaining to the final conflict.

Let us first widen our contextual lens with a prophetic Psalm of David which provides a broad overview of the time leading up to the final conflict at the end of the age. The nations are gathering to fight against the Lord of Hosts. They are in such deep deception, that they actually think they can defeat our Lord and Savior.

> *Why do the nations conspire and the peoples plot in vain? The kings of the earth rise up and the rulers band together against the Lord and against his anointed, saying, "Let us break their chains and throw off their shackles." The One enthroned in heaven laughs; the Lord scoffs at them. He rebukes them in his anger and terrifies them in his wrath, saying, "I have installed my king on Zion, my holy mountain." I will proclaim the Lord's decree: He said to me, "You are my son; today I have become your father. Ask me, and I will make the nations your inheritance, the ends of the earth your possession. You will break them with a rod of iron; you will dash them to pieces like pottery." Therefore, you kings, be wise; be warned, you rulers of the earth. Serve the Lord with fear and celebrate his rule with trembling. Kiss his son, or he will be angry and your way will lead to your destruction, for his wrath can flare up in a moment. Blessed are all who take refuge in him. (Psalm 2)*

Now that the stage is set, let's focus in on the final battle, reviewing several scriptures that describe the scene.

The Heavenly Warrior Defeats the Beast

I saw heaven standing open and there before me was a white horse, whose rider is called Faithful and True. With justice he judges and wages war. His eyes are like blazing fire, and on his head are many crowns. He has a name written on him that no one knows but he himself. He is dressed in a robe dipped in blood, and his name is the Word of God. The armies of heaven were following him, riding on white horses and dressed in fine linen, white and clean. Coming out of his mouth is a sharp sword with which to strike down the nations. "He will rule them with an iron scepter." [See also Genesis 49:10, Numbers 24:17, Psalm 45:6, Hebrews 1:8, Psalm 110:2, Micah 7:14 & Revelation 12:5]. He treads the winepress of the fury of the wrath of God Almighty. On his robe and on his thigh he has this name written:

KING OF KINGS AND LORD OF LORDS.

And I saw an angel standing in the sun, who cried in a loud voice to all the birds flying in midair, "Come, gather together for the great supper of God, so that you may eat the flesh of kings, generals, and the mighty, of horses and their riders, and the flesh of all people, free and slave, great and small."

Then I saw the beast and the kings of the earth and their armies gathered together to wage war against the rider on the horse and his army. But the beast was captured, and with it the false prophet who had performed the signs on its behalf. With these signs he had deluded those who had received the mark of the beast and worshiped its image. The two of them were thrown alive into the fiery lake of burning sulfur. The rest were killed with the sword coming out of the mouth of the rider on the horse, and all the birds gorged themselves on their flesh. (Revelation 19:11-21)

The Lord says to my lord: "Sit at my right hand until I make your enemies a footstool for your feet." The Lord will extend your mighty scepter from Zion, saying, "Rule in the midst of your enemies!" Your troops will be willing on your day of battle. Arrayed in holy splendor, your young men will come to you like dew from the morning's

*womb. The Lord has sworn and will not change his mind:
"You are a priest forever, in the order of Melchizedek."
The Lord is at your right hand; he will crush kings on the
day of his wrath. He will judge the nations, heaping up
the dead and crushing the rulers of the whole earth. He
will drink from a brook along the way, and so he will lift
his head high. (Psalm 110)*

*Before your pots can feel the heat of the thorns—
whether they be green or dry—the wicked will be swept
away. The righteous will be glad when they are avenged,
when they dip their feet in the blood of the wicked. Then
people will say, "Surely the righteous still are rewarded;
surely there is a God who judges the earth." (Psalm 58:9-
11)*

God's Day of Vengeance and Redemption

*Who is this coming from Edom, from Bozrah, with his
garments stained crimson? Who is this, robed in
splendor, striding forward in the greatness of his
strength? "It is I, proclaiming victory, mighty to save."
Why are your garments red, like those of one treading
the winepress? "I have trodden the winepress alone;
from the nations no one was with me. I trampled them in
my anger and trod them down in my wrath; their blood
spattered my garments, and I stained all my clothing. It
was for me the day of vengeance; the year for me to
redeem had come. I looked, but there was no one to help,
I was appalled that no one gave support; so my own arm
achieved salvation for me, and my own wrath sustained
me. I trampled the nations in my anger; in my wrath I
made them drunk and poured their blood on the
ground." (Isaiah 63:1-6)*

"On that day," declares the Lord, "a cry will go up from the Fish Gate, wailing from the New Quarter, and a loud crash from the hills. Wail, you who live in the market district; all your merchants will be wiped out, all who trade with silver will be destroyed. At that time I will search Jerusalem with lamps and punish those who are complacent, who are like wine left on its dregs, who think, 'The Lord will do nothing, either good or bad.' Their wealth will be plundered, their houses demolished. Though they build houses, they will not live in them; though they plant vineyards, they will not drink the wine."

The great day of the Lord is near—near and coming quickly. The cry on the day of the Lord is bitter; the Mighty Warrior shouts his battle cry. That day will be a day of wrath—a day of distress and anguish, a day of trouble and ruin, a day of darkness and gloom, a day of clouds and blackness—a day of trumpet and battle cry against the fortified cities and against the corner towers.

"I will bring such distress on all people that they will grope about like those who are blind, because they have sinned against the Lord. Their blood will be poured out like dust and their entrails like dung. Neither their silver nor their gold will be able to save them on the day of the Lord's wrath." (Zephaniah 1:10-18)

"Let the nations be roused; let them advance into the Valley of Jehoshaphat, for there I will sit to judge all the nations on every side. Swing the sickle, for the harvest is ripe. Come, trample the grapes, for the winepress is full and the vats overflow—so great is their wickedness!"

Multitudes, multitudes in the valley of decision! For the

day of the Lord is near in the valley of decision. The sun and moon will be darkened, and the stars no longer shine. The Lord will roar from Zion and thunder from Jerusalem; the earth and the heavens will tremble. But the Lord will be a refuge for his people, a stronghold for the people of Israel. (Joel 3:12-16)

How great, awesome, terrible, wonderful, beautiful and mysterious is the great Day of the Lord! It stretches the bounds of the imagination! The Word of God promises that this will be a day of great rejoicing for the saints who have long awaiting the Bridegroom's return. Let us be encouraged to know that there will be great rejoicing, even in the midst of the battle!

Sing to the Lord a new song, his praise in the assembly of his faithful people. Let Israel rejoice in their Maker; let the people of Zion be glad in their King. Let them praise his name with dancing and make music to him with timbrel and harp. For the Lord takes delight in his people; he crowns the humble with victory. Let his faithful people rejoice in this honor and sing for joy on their beds. May the praise of God be in their mouths and a double-edged sword in their hands, to inflict vengeance on the nations and punishment on the peoples, to bind their kings with fetters, their nobles with shackles of iron, to carry out the sentence written against them—this is the glory of all his faithful people. Praise the Lord. (Psalm 149:1-7)

13 | HEADING BACK TO PARADISE WITH THE KING OF GLORY

As Jesus returns to avenge His Bride, we see an amazing transition from the final conflict to a joyful procession. One very descriptive picture of this transition can be found in chapters 34 and 35 of Isaiah.

Judgment Against the Nations

Come near, you nations, and listen; pay attention, you peoples! Let the earth hear, and all that is in it, the world, and all that comes out of it! The Lord is angry with all nations; his wrath is on all their armies. He will totally destroy them, he will give them over to slaughter. Their slain will be thrown out, their dead bodies will stink; the mountains will be soaked with their blood. All the stars in the sky will be dissolved and the heavens rolled up like a scroll; all the starry host will fall like withered leaves from the vine, like shriveled figs from the fig tree. My sword has drunk its fill in the heavens; see, it descends in judgment on Edom, the people I have totally destroyed. The sword of the Lord is bathed in blood, it is covered with fat—the blood of lambs and goats, fat from the kidneys of rams. For the Lord has a sacrifice in Bozrah and a great slaughter in the land of Edom. And the wild oxen will fall with them, the bull calves and the great bulls. Their land will be drenched with blood, and the dust will be soaked with fat. For the Lord has a day of vengeance, a year of retribution, to uphold Zion's cause. Edom's streams will be turned into pitch, her dust into burning sulfur; her land will become blazing pitch! It will not be quenched night or day; its smoke will rise forever. From generation to generation it will lie desolate; no one will ever pass through it again. The desert owl and screech owl will possess it; the great owl and the raven will nest there. God will stretch out over Edom the measuring line of chaos and the plumb line of desolation. Her nobles will have nothing there to be called a kingdom, all her princes will vanish away. Thorns will overrun her citadels, nettles and brambles her strongholds. She will become a haunt for jackals, a home for owls. Desert creatures will meet with hyenas, and wild goats will bleat to each other; there the night creatures will also lie down and find for themselves places of rest. The owl will nest there and lay eggs, she will hatch them, and care for her young under the shadow of her wings; there also the falcons will gather, each with its mate. Look in the scroll of the Lord and read:

None of these will be missing,
  not one will lack her mate.
For it is his mouth that has given the order,
  and his Spirit will gather them together.

He allots their portions;
  his hand distributes them by measure.

> *They will possess it forever*
> *and dwell there from generation to generation.*

Joy of the Redeemed

The desert and the parched land will be glad; the wilderness will rejoice and blossom. Like the crocus, it will burst into bloom; it will rejoice greatly and shout for joy. The glory of Lebanon will be given to it, the splendor of Carmel and Sharon; they will see the glory of the Lord, the splendor of our God. Strengthen the feeble hands, steady the knees that give way; say to those with fearful hearts, "Be strong, do not fear; your God will come, he will come with vengeance; with divine retribution he will come to save you." Then will the eyes of the blind be opened and the ears of the deaf unstopped. Then will the lame leap like a deer, and the mute tongue shout for joy. Water will gush forth in the wilderness and streams in the desert. The burning sand will become a pool, the thirsty ground bubbling springs. In the haunts where jackals once lay, grass and reeds and papyrus will grow. And a highway will be there; it will be called the Way of Holiness; it will be for those who walk on that Way. The unclean will not journey on it; wicked fools will not go about on it. No lion will be there, nor any ravenous beast; they will not be found there. But only the redeemed will walk there, and those the Lord has rescued will return. They will enter Zion with singing; everlasting joy will crown their heads. Gladness and joy will overtake them, and sorrow and sighing will flee away. (Isaiah 34 & 35)

Surrounding the return of our Savior, Bridegroom and King, we see the unveiling of a procession.

Deliverance Promised

"I will surely gather all of you, Jacob; I will surely bring together the remnant of Israel. I will bring them together like sheep in a pen, like a flock in its pasture; the place will throng with people. The One who breaks open the way will go up before them; they will break through the gate and go out. Their King will pass through before them, the Lord at their head." (Micah 2:12-13)

This is what the Lord says: "Sing with joy for Jacob; shout for the foremost of the nations. Make your praises heard, and say, 'Lord, save your people, the remnant of Israel.' See, I will bring them from the land of the north and gather them from the ends of the earth. Among them will be the blind and the lame, expectant mothers and women in labor; a great throng will return. They will come with weeping; they will pray as I bring them back. I will lead them beside streams of water on a level path where they will not stumble, because I am Israel's father, and Ephraim is my firstborn son. Hear the word of the Lord, you nations; proclaim it in distant coastlands: 'He who scattered Israel will gather them and will watch over his flock like a shepherd.' For the Lord will deliver Jacob and redeem them from the hand of those stronger than they. They will come and shout for joy on the heights of Zion; they will rejoice in the bounty of the Lord—the grain, the new wine and the olive oil, the young of the flocks and herds. They will be like a well-watered garden, and they will sorrow no more. Then young women will dance and be glad, young men and old as well. I will turn their mourning into gladness; I will give them comfort and joy instead of sorrow. I will satisfy the priests with abundance, and my people will be filled with my bounty," declares the Lord. (Jeremiah 31:7-14)

"Since you are precious and honored in my sight, and because I love you, I will give people in exchange for you, nations in exchange for your life. Do not be afraid, for I am with you; I will bring your children from the east and gather you from the west. I will say to the north, 'Give them up!' and to the south, 'Do not hold them back.' Bring my sons from afar and my daughters from the ends of the earth—everyone who is called by my name, whom I created for my glory, whom I formed and made."

Lead out those who have eyes but are blind, who have ears but are deaf. All the nations gather together and the peoples assemble. Which of their gods foretold this and proclaimed to us the former things? Let them bring in their witnesses to prove they were right, so that others may hear and say, "It is true." "You are my witnesses," declares the Lord, "and my servant whom I have chosen, so that you may know and believe me and understand that I am he. Before me no god was formed, nor will there be one after me. I, even I, am the Lord, and apart from me there is no savior. I have revealed and saved and proclaimed—I, and not some foreign god among you. You are my witnesses," declares the Lord, "that I am God. Yes, and from ancient days I am he. No one can deliver out of my hand. When I act, who can reverse it?" (Isaiah 43:4-13)

Your procession, God, has come into view, the procession of my God and King into the sanctuary. In front are the singers, after them the musicians; with them are the young women playing the timbrels. Praise God in the great congregation; praise the Lord in the assembly of Israel. There is the little tribe of Benjamin, leading them, there the great throng of Judah's princes, and there the princes of Zebulun and of Naphtali.

Summon your power, God; show us your strength, our God, as you have done before. Because of your temple at Jerusalem kings will bring you gifts. Rebuke the beast among the reeds, the herd of bulls among the calves of the nations. Humbled, may the beast bring bars of silver. Scatter the nations who delight in war. Envoys will come from Egypt; Cush will submit herself to God.

Sing to God, you kingdoms of the earth, sing praise to the Lord, to him who rides across the highest heavens, the ancient heavens, who thunders with mighty voice. Proclaim the power of God, whose majesty is over Israel, whose power is in the heavens. You, God, are awesome in your sanctuary; the God of Israel gives power and strength to his people. Praise be to God! (Psalm 68:24-35)

When will this procession happen? It will happen when Jesus returns; it will begin when we go out to meet Him! We will welcome Him back, joining Him in war and in procession. These events will begin to unfold upon the sounding of the final trumpet.

"Then will appear the sign of the Son of Man in heaven. And then all the peoples of the earth will mourn when they see the Son of Man coming on the clouds of heaven, with power and great glory. And he will send his angels with a loud trumpet call, and they will gather his elect

from the four winds, from one end of the heavens to the
other." *(Matthew 24:30-31)*

Paul refers to the gathering of the saints to go out to meet
our Bridegroom *(Apantesis)* in terms of the welcoming of a
dignitary at His coming *(Parousia)*.

*According to the Lord's word, we tell you that we who
are still alive, who are left until the coming of the Lord,
will certainly not precede those who have fallen asleep.
For the Lord himself will come down from heaven, with a
loud command, with the voice of the archangel and with
the trumpet call of God, and the dead in Christ will rise
first. After that, we who are still alive and are left will be
caught up together with them in the clouds to meet the
Lord in the air. And so we will be with the Lord forever.
(1 Thessalonians 4:15-17)*

*"At midnight the cry rang out: 'Here's the bridegroom!
Come out to meet him!'" (Matthew 25:6)*

Once Jesus and His beloved saints win the great conflict of
the ages, and once they all return to Jerusalem, there will be
some feasting and celebrating to do! There will also be a
reckoning appointed for those who opposed Him.

*"In that day the Lord will thresh from the flowing
Euphrates to the Wadi of Egypt, and you, Israel, will be
gathered up one by one. And in that day a great trumpet
will sound. Those who were perishing in Assyria and
those who were exiled in Egypt will come and worship
the Lord on the holy mountain in Jerusalem." (Isaiah
27:12-13)*

The Nations Judged

"In those days and at that time, when I restore the fortunes of Judah and Jerusalem, I will gather all nations and bring them down to the Valley of Jehoshaphat. There I will put them on trial for what they did to my inheritance, my people Israel, because they scattered my people among the nations and divided up my land. They cast lots for my people and traded boys for prostitutes; they sold girls for wine to drink." (Joel 3:1-3)

The Sheep and the Goats

"When the Son of Man comes in his glory, and all the angels with him, he will sit on his glorious throne. All the nations will be gathered before him, and he will separate the people one from another as a shepherd separates the sheep from the goats. He will put the sheep on his right and the goats on his left. Then the King will say to those on his right, 'Come, you who are blessed by my Father; take your inheritance, the kingdom prepared for you since the creation of the world. For I was hungry and you gave me something to eat, I was thirsty and you gave me something to drink, I was a stranger and you invited me in, I needed clothes and you clothed me, I was sick and you looked after me, I was in prison and you came to visit me.' Then the righteous will answer him, 'Lord, when did we see you hungry and feed you, or thirsty and give you something to drink? When did we see you a stranger and invite you in, or needing clothes and clothe you? When did we see you sick or in prison and go to visit you?' The King will reply, 'Truly I tell you, whatever you did for one of the least of these brothers and sisters of mine, you did for me.' Then he will say to those on his left, 'Depart from me, you who are cursed, into the

eternal fire prepared for the devil and his angels. For I was hungry and you gave me nothing to eat, I was thirsty and you gave me nothing to drink, I was a stranger and you did not invite me in, I needed clothes and you did not clothe me, I was sick and in prison and you did not look after me.' They also will answer, 'Lord, when did we see you hungry or thirsty or a stranger or needing clothes or sick or in prison, and did not help you?' He will reply, 'Truly I tell you, whatever you did not do for one of the least of these, you did not do for me.' Then they will go away to eternal punishment, but the righteous to eternal life." (Matthew 25:31-46)

"This is what the Lord says: 'I will restore the fortunes of Jacob's tents and have compassion on his dwellings; the city will be rebuilt on her ruins, and the palace will stand in its proper place. From them will come songs of thanksgiving and the sound of rejoicing. I will add to their numbers, and they will not be decreased; I will bring them honor, and they will not be disdained. Their children will be as in days of old, and their community will be established before me; I will punish all who oppress them. Their leader will be one of their own; their ruler will arise from among them. I will bring him near and he will come close to me—for who is he who will devote himself to be close to me?' declares the Lord. 'So you will be my people, and I will be your God.' See, the storm of the Lord will burst out in wrath, a driving wind swirling down on the heads of the wicked. The fierce anger of the Lord will not turn back until he fully accomplishes the purposes of his heart. In days to come you will understand this." (Jeremiah 30:18-34)

"The days are coming," declares the Lord, "when I will

make a new covenant with the people of Israel and with the people of Judah. It will not be like the covenant I made with their ancestors when I took them by the hand to lead them out of Egypt, because they broke my covenant, though I was a husband to them," declares the Lord. "This is the covenant I will make with the people of Israel after that time," declares the Lord. "I will put my law in their minds and write it on their hearts. I will be their God, and they will be my people. No longer will they teach their neighbor, or say to one another, 'Know the Lord,' because they will all know me, from the least of them to the greatest," declares the Lord. "For I will forgive their wickedness and will remember their sins no more."

This is what the Lord says, he who appoints the sun to shine by day, who decrees the moon and stars to shine by night, who stirs up the sea so that its waves roar—the Lord Almighty is his name: "Only if these decrees vanish from my sight," declares the Lord, "will Israel ever cease being a nation before me."

This is what the Lord says: "Only if the heavens above can be measured and the foundations of the earth below be searched out will I reject all the descendants of Israel because of all they have done," declares the Lord.

"The days are coming," declares the Lord, "when this city will be rebuilt for me from the Tower of Hananel to the Corner Gate. The measuring line will stretch from there straight to the hill of Gareb and then turn to Goah. The whole valley where dead bodies and ashes are thrown, and all the terraces out to the Kidron Valley on the east as far as the corner of the Horse Gate, will be holy to the Lord. The city will never again be uprooted or

demolished." (Jeremiah 31:31-40)

On this mountain the Lord Almighty will prepare a feast of rich food for all peoples, a banquet of aged wine—the best of meats and the finest of wines. On this mountain he will destroy the shroud that enfolds all peoples, the sheet that covers all nations; he will swallow up death forever. The Sovereign Lord will wipe away the tears from all faces; he will remove his people's disgrace from all the earth. The Lord has spoken. In that day they will say, "Surely this is our God; we trusted in him, and he saved us. This is the Lord, we trusted in him; let us rejoice and be glad in his salvation." (Isaiah 25:6-9)

"Be dressed ready for service and keep your lamps burning, like servants waiting for their master to return from a wedding banquet, so that when he comes and knocks they can immediately open the door for him. It will be good for those servants whose master finds them watching when he comes. Truly I tell you, he will dress himself to serve, will have them recline at the table and will come and wait on them." (Luke 12:35-37)

Then I heard what sounded like a great multitude, like the roar of rushing waters and like loud peals of thunder, shouting: "Hallelujah! For our Lord God Almighty reigns. Let us rejoice and be glad and give him glory! For the wedding of the Lamb has come, and his bride has made herself ready. Fine linen, bright and clean, was given her to wear." (Fine linen stands for the righteous acts of God's holy people.) Then the angel said to me, "Write this: Blessed are those who are invited to the wedding supper of the Lamb!" And he added, "These are the true words of God." (Revelation 19:6-9)

14 | THE REWARDS OF THE OVERCOMER

What a privilege it is for us to be born into the world for such a time as this! I couldn't think of a more exciting time to be alive. *Jesus looked throughout history and handpicked us specifically to be alive during this generation!* Part of our inheritance is that of the overcomer. He set this whole thing up so that we'd have an enemy to take out. He set it up so that we would: 1) grow in the process of battling and overcoming the enemy, 2) receive great rewards for doing so, and 3) so that His precious and mighty Name would be glorified in the process. Sometimes it is better to just be quiet and let God talk. So, let us now allow Abba Father to encourage us and speak to us tenderly through the Holy Spirit in regards to our inheritance as overcomers.

For though the mountains should depart and the hills be shaken or removed, yet My love and kindness shall not depart from you, nor shall My covenant of peace and completeness be removed, says the Lord, Who has compassion on you. O you afflicted [city], storm-tossed and not comforted, behold, I will set your stones in fair colors [in antimony to enhance their brilliance] and lay your foundations with sapphires. And I will make your windows and pinnacles of [sparkling] agates or rubies, and your gates of [shining] carbuncles, and all your walls [of your enclosures] of precious stones. And all your [spiritual] children shall be disciples [taught by the Lord and obedient to His will], and great shall be the peace and undisturbed composure of your children. You shall establish yourself in righteousness (rightness, in conformity with God's will and order): you shall be far from even the thought of oppression or destruction, for you shall not fear, and from terror, for it shall not come near you. Behold, they may gather together and stir up strife, but it is not from Me. Whoever stirs up strife against you shall fall and surrender to you. Behold, I have created the smith who blows on the fire of coals and who produces a weapon for its purpose; and I have created the devastator to destroy. But no weapon that is formed against you shall prosper, and every tongue that shall rise against you in judgment you shall show to be in the wrong. This [peace, righteousness, security, triumph over opposition] is the heritage of the servants of the Lord [those in whom the ideal Servant of the Lord is reproduced]; this is the righteousness or the vindication which they obtain from Me [this is that which I impart to them as their justification], says the Lord. (Isaiah 54:10-17, AMP)

"I will build my church, and the gates of Hades will not overcome it." (Matthew 16:18)

The light shines in the darkness, and the darkness has not overcome it. (John 1:5)

"In this world you will have trouble. But take heart! I have overcome the world." (John 16:33)

Do not be overcome by evil, but overcome evil with good. (Romans 12:21)

You, dear children, are from God and have overcome them, because the one who is in you is greater than the one who is in the world. (I John 4:4)

...for everyone born of God overcomes the world. This is the victory that has overcome the world, even our faith. Who is it that overcomes the world? Only the one who believes that Jesus is the Son of God. (I John 5:4-5)

"He who has an ear, let him hear what the Spirit says to the churches. To him who overcomes, I will grant to eat of the tree of life which is in the Paradise of God." (Revelation 2:7, NASB)

"He who has an ear, let him hear what the Spirit says to the churches. He who overcomes will not be hurt by the second death." (Revelation 2:11, NASB)

"He who has an ear, let him hear what the Spirit says to the churches. To him who overcomes, to him I will give some of the hidden manna, and I will give him a white stone, and a new name written on the stone which no one knows but he who receives it." (Revelation 2:17, NASB)

"He who overcomes, and he who keeps My deeds until the end, to him I will give authority over the nations..." (Revelation 2:26, NASB)

"He who overcomes will thus be clothed in white garments; and I will not erase his name from the book of life, and I will confess his name before My Father and before His angels." (Revelation 3:5, NASB)

"He who overcomes, I will make him a pillar in the temple of My God, and he will not go out from it anymore; and I will write on him the name of My God, and the name of the city of My God, the new Jerusalem, which comes down out of heaven from My God, and My new name." (Revelation 3:12, NASB)

"He who overcomes, I will grant to him to sit down with Me on My throne, as I also overcame and sat down with My Father on His throne." (Revelation 3:21, NASB)

"He who overcomes will inherit these things, and I will be his God and he will be My son." (Revelation 21:17, NASB)

Then I saw thrones, and they sat on them, and judgment was given to them. And I saw the souls of those who had been beheaded because of their testimony of Jesus and because of the word of God, and those who had not worshiped the beast or his image, and had not received the mark on their forehead and on their hand; and they came to life and reigned with Christ for a thousand years. (Revelation 20:4, NASB)

Many evils confront the [consistently] righteous, but the Lord delivers him out of them all. (Psalm 34:19, AMP)

He replied, "I saw Satan fall like lightning from heaven. I have given you authority to trample on snakes and scorpions and to overcome all the power of the enemy; nothing will harm you. However, do not rejoice that the spirits submit to you, but rejoice that your names are written in heaven." (Luke 18:20)

And they overcame him [Satan] because of the blood of the Lamb and because of the word of their testimony, and they did not love their life even when faced with death. (Revelation 12:11, NASB)

The God of peace will soon crush Satan under your feet. The grace of our Lord Jesus be with you. (Romans 16:20, NASB)

Because God wanted to make the unchanging nature of his purpose very clear to the heirs of what was promised, he confirmed it with an oath. God did this so that, by two unchangeable things in which it is impossible for God to lie, we who have fled to take hold of the hope set before us may be greatly encouraged. We have this hope as an anchor for the soul, firm and secure. It enters the inner sanctuary behind the curtain, where our forerunner, Jesus, has entered on our behalf. He has become a high priest forever, in the order of Melchizedek. (Hebrews 6:17-20)

15 | THE TIMES AND SEASONS

Jesus commanded us to study and know the times and seasons. Jesus admonished the Pharisees and Sadducees for not being able to recognize the signs of the times. That is why they missed the Messiah, even though He was standing right in front of them.

The Pharisees and Sadducees came to Jesus and tested him by asking him to show them a sign from heaven. He replied, "When evening comes, you say, 'It will be fair weather, for the sky is red,' and in the morning, 'Today it will be stormy, for the sky is red and overcast.' You know how to interpret the appearance of the sky, but you cannot interpret the signs of the times." (Matthew 16:1-3)

As he approached Jerusalem and saw the city, he wept over it and said, "If you, even you, had only known on this day what would bring you peace—but now it is hidden from your eyes. The days will come upon you when your enemies will build an embankment against you and encircle you and hem you in on every side. They will dash you to the ground, you and the children within your walls. They will not leave one stone on another, because you did not recognize the time of God's coming to you." (Luke 19:41-44)

We find clear warnings about the end times all throughout the Bible. Indeed there is much more information throughout the Old and New Testaments about the events surrounding the second coming of Christ than there is about His first advent. Jesus himself laid out a clear overview of the end times in the Bible and expects us to read it and to seek Him to understand it. In regards to the end times, Jesus said, *"See, I have told you ahead of time"* (Matthew 24:26). Jesus also made one of the strongest qualifying statements that He ever made when He was speaking about what would happen in the end times. He said, *"Heaven and earth will pass away, but my words will never pass away"* (Matthew 24:35). Yet, we know from the words of Jesus that despite these many warnings, many religious and God fearing people, as well as many unbelievers, will still be unaware and caught off guard. Let us not miss the times and seasons! Let us always watch, pray and keep our lamp burning. Let us always, with great patience and endurance, passionately and compassionately carry out what He has for us to do in these coming days.

I believe one of the simplest and easiest ways to obtain a high level overview of the end times is to read Jesus' discourse on the end times in the Gospels. Once we have read these scriptures, with the help of the Holy Spirit, a foundation will be laid. Then, as the rest of the prophetic writings in the Bible are explored, they will begin to be understood with increasing clarity and precision.

Most of Jesus' discourse on the end times can be found in Matthew 13, 24 & 25; Mark 13 and Luke 17 & 21. The largest scriptural passage on the subject is found in Matthew 24 & 25. In Appendix B of this book, I have spliced together all of Jesus' primary end times discourse. I used Matthew 13, 24 & 25 as the foundation, including any additional passages or phrases, in chronological order, that were not included in those three chapters (with their respective references). I would recommend that you take some time to read through those passages. For the sake of simplicity, I have included Matthew 24 below. We will start in Matthew 24 by reviewing Jesus' description of the end times and His instructions about what we should be watching for. The chapter begins with the disciples asking Jesus about the timing of the destruction of the temple (which happened subsequently in c. 70 AD) and about the time of His coming and the end of the age.

Matthew Chapter 24

The Destruction of the Temple and Signs of the End Times

Jesus left the temple and was walking away when his disciples came up to him to call his attention to its buildings. "Do you see all these things?" he asked. "Truly I tell you, not one stone here will be left on another; every one will be thrown down."

As Jesus was sitting on the Mount of Olives, the disciples came to him privately. "Tell us," they said, "when will this happen, and what will be the sign of your coming and of the end of the age?"

Jesus answered: "Watch out that no one deceives you. For many will come in my name, claiming, 'I am the Messiah,' and will deceive many. You will hear of wars and rumors of wars, but see to it that you are not alarmed. Such things must happen, but the end is still to come. Nation will rise against nation, and kingdom against kingdom. There will be famines and earthquakes in various places. All these are the beginning of birth pains.

"Then you will be handed over to be persecuted and put to death, and you will be hated by all nations because of me. At that time many will turn away from the faith and will betray and hate each other, and many false prophets will appear and deceive many people. Because of the increase of wickedness, the love of most will grow cold, but the one who stands firm to the end will be saved. And this gospel of the kingdom will be preached in the whole world as a testimony to all nations, and then the end will come.

"So when you see standing in the holy place 'the abomination that causes desolation,' spoken of through the prophet Daniel—let the reader understand—then let those who are in Judea flee to the mountains. Let no one on the housetop go down to take anything out of the house. Let no one in the field go back to get their cloak. How dreadful it will be in those days for pregnant women and nursing mothers! Pray that your flight will not take place in winter or on the Sabbath. For then there will be great distress, unequaled from the beginning of the world until now—and never to be equaled again.

"If those days had not been cut short, no one would survive, but for the sake of the elect those days will be shortened. At that time if anyone says to you, 'Look, here is the Messiah!' or, 'There he is!' do not believe it. For

false messiahs and false prophets will appear and perform great signs and wonders to deceive, if possible, even the elect. See, I have told you ahead of time.

"So if anyone tells you, 'There he is, out in the wilderness,' do not go out; or, 'Here he is, in the inner rooms,' do not believe it. For as lightning that comes from the east is visible even in the west, so will be the coming of the Son of Man. Wherever there is a carcass, there the vultures will gather.

   "Immediately after the distress of those days

   "'the sun will be darkened,
     and the moon will not give its light;
   the stars will fall from the sky,
     and the heavenly bodies will be shaken.'

"Then will appear the sign of the Son of Man in heaven. And then all the peoples of the earth will mourn when they see the Son of Man coming on the clouds of heaven, with power and great glory. And he will send his angels with a loud trumpet call, and they will gather his elect from the four winds, from one end of the heavens to the other.

"Now learn this lesson from the fig tree: As soon as its twigs get tender and its leaves come out, you know that summer is near. Even so, when you see all these things, you know that it is near, right at the door. Truly I tell you, this generation will certainly not pass away until all these things have happened. Heaven and earth will pass away, but my words will never pass away.

The Day and Hour Unknown

"But about that day or hour no one knows, not even the

angels in heaven, nor the Son, but only the Father. As it was in the days of Noah, so it will be at the coming of the Son of Man. For in the days before the flood, people were eating and drinking, marrying and giving in marriage, up to the day Noah entered the ark; and they knew nothing about what would happen until the flood came and took them all away. That is how it will be at the coming of the Son of Man. Two men will be in the field; one will be taken and the other left. Two women will be grinding with a hand mill; one will be taken and the other left.

"Therefore keep watch, because you do not know on what day your Lord will come. But understand this: If the owner of the house had known at what time of night the thief was coming, he would have kept watch and would not have let his house be broken into. So you also must be ready, because the Son of Man will come at an hour when you do not expect him.

"Who then is the faithful and wise servant, whom the master has put in charge of the servants in his household to give them their food at the proper time? It will be good for that servant whose master finds him doing so when he returns. Truly I tell you, he will put him in charge of all his possessions. But suppose that servant is wicked and says to himself, 'My master is staying away a long time,' and he then begins to beat his fellow servants and to eat and drink with drunkards. The master of that servant will come on a day when he does not expect him and at an hour he is not aware of. He will cut him to pieces and assign him a place with the hypocrites, where there will be weeping and gnashing of teeth." (Matthew 24)

Things We Know, Things We Think We Know and Things We Don't Know

Once again, the goal of this book is to explore the Father's heart and purpose for the end times, not to go into painstaking detail about different and widely varying perspectives on the exact timing of all of the peripheral events surrounding the end times. I strongly believe it is much more critical for each of us to continue seeking the Lord, staying in constant relationship with Him—continually praying, worshipping and studying the Word of God and asking the Holy Spirit for guidance and revelation about the end times—than to spend the majority of our time searching out the details of the eschatological perspectives of mere humans.

I recall as I began to search through scriptures regarding the end times, I was getting a little frustrated about the timing of the seals, trumpets and bowls of wrath. So, one day I did an internet search for an image of an eschatological timeline. About fifty timelines popped up right away. Guess what? They were all different! Right then I had my answer. There are no short-cuts! Beloved, there is no book written by any individual, including myself, that will explain everything about the end times. Honestly, I think you would have a similar experience to what I had with the timelines, if you tried to find a good book to explain every detail about the how the end times will unfold. The viewpoints are going to be all over the place. There are thousands of books on the subject. And don't get me wrong, many of these books are written by God-fearing believers. Many of the authors are oaks of righteousness. They should be respected and commended for their faith. They are gifted, intelligent people, many with advanced degrees in their fields of study.

However, it doesn't take a math major to figure out that if there are many different viewpoints on a subject, very few of these viewpoints (if any) contain the full, complete and accurate revelation. For example, if you only had two major end time theories, at least half of them would be wrong! With so many end time theories, it follows that the bulk of the detail that has been written on the subject has some level of error in it. There is only one Book that has it right. As you probably, know I am talking about the Bible, the Word of God—the final word on the subject! We should determine to spend most of our time in the Bible, creating a foundation. We should be judging any other end time book that we happen to read by the Word of God, rather than judging the Holy Scriptures by some book or opinion written by a mere human being.

We can't enter the Kingdom of God by knowing someone who knows God, let alone someone who says they know God. We must each know God for ourselves and build a personal relationship with Him. This includes having real discussions with Him about the times in which we live and the times which are to come (see John 16:13). We must individually wrestle with God about this topic, instead of ignoring the subject or picking an item off of the "end times menu" of personal or theological opinion.

So, my prayer is that we can all explore this individually and also together. Let us dwell together in unity under Christ, seeking and asking the Holy Spirit to continue to reveal these things to us in His perfect timing. Let us love and honor one another in the meantime, realizing that many of the details of what is yet to come are yet to be revealed. And I pray that we all become willing to accept the truth of His Word as it is revealed to us.

"How good and pleasant it is when God's people live together in unity! It is like precious oil poured on the head, running down on the beard, running down on Aaron's beard, down on the collar of his robe. It is as if the dew of Hermon were falling on Mount Zion. For there the Lord bestows his blessing, even life forevermore." (Psalm 133:1-3)

All that said, I will only cover a few items in this chapter that I believe are things we can see plainly in the Scripture, some things that appear to be clear from the Scripture and some other things that aren't made clear in the Scripture. Then, I will make a few personal observations. I would ask you to do the same. Please don't take any of this at face value. Like a good Berean, I would encourage you to search it out for yourself. If you can't find it in the Bible, throw it out! We should individually watch, pray and seek the Lord to discern the times and seasons. We should also meet together, sharing and encouraging each other about these things—always honoring and praying for one another. Let us live out our days with grace and with the fruit of the Holy Spirit.

Some Things We Know from Scripture

1. Jesus Christ is returning for His Bride!

    *   I have included a long reading list in Appendix A for you to explore if you are interested. The return of Jesus Christ is found throughout the Word of God— from Genesis to Revelation. For example, Jesus said, *"Then will appear the sign of the Son of Man in heaven. And then all the peoples of the earth will mourn when they see the Son of Man coming on the clouds of heaven, with power and great glory"* (Matthew 24:30).

159

2.   When Jesus returns, every eye will see Him

- *"And then all the peoples of the earth will mourn when they see the Son of Man coming on the clouds of heaven, with power and great glory." (Matthew 24:30)*

- *Then he said to his disciples, "The time is coming when you will long to see one of the days of the Son of Man, but you will not see it. People will tell you, 'There he is!' or 'Here he is!' Do not go running off after them. For the Son of Man in his day will be like the lightning, which flashes and lights up the sky from one end to the other." (Luke 17:22-24)*

- *"Look, he is coming with the clouds," and "every eye will see him, even those who pierced him"; and all peoples on earth "will mourn because of him." So shall it be! Amen. (Revelation 1:7)*

3.   Jesus' return will occur after a time of great deception and persecution

- *Jesus answered: "Watch out that no one deceives you. For many will come in my name, claiming, 'I am the Messiah,' and will deceive many." (Matthew 24:4-5)*

- *"Then you will be handed over to be persecuted and put to death, and you will be hated by all nations because of me. At that time many will turn away from the faith and will betray and hate each other, and many false prophets will appear and deceive many people. Because of the increase of wickedness, the love of most will grow cold, but the one who stands firm to the end will be saved." (Matthew 24:9-13)*

- *After this I looked, and there before me was a great*

> multitude that no one could count, from every nation, tribe, people and language, standing before the throne and before the Lamb...
>
> ...And he said, "These are they who have come out of the great tribulation; they have washed their robes and made them white in the blood of the Lamb." (Revelation 7:9,14)

4.   Jesus' return will occur after a time when many nations once again surround, besiege and war against Jerusalem

- *"When you see Jerusalem being surrounded by armies, you will know that its desolation is near. Then let those who are in Judea flee to the mountains, let those in the city get out, and let those in the country not enter the city. For this is the time of punishment in fulfillment of all that has been written." (Luke 21:20-22)*

- *A prophecy: The word of the Lord concerning Israel. The Lord, who stretches out the heavens, who lays the foundation of the earth, and who forms the human spirit within a person, declares: "I am going to make Jerusalem a cup that sends all the surrounding peoples reeling. Judah will be besieged as well as Jerusalem. On that day, when all the nations of the earth are gathered against her, I will make Jerusalem an immovable rock for all the nations. All who try to move it will injure themselves." (Zechariah 12:1-3)*

5.   Jesus' return will occur after a time of greatly increased evangelism and harvest

- *"Because of the increase of wickedness, the love of most will grow cold, but the one who stands firm to the end will be saved. And this gospel of the kingdom will be preached in the whole world as a testimony to all nations, and then the end will come." (Matthew 24:12-14)*

- *The sun will be turned to darkness and the moon to blood before the coming of the great and dreadful day of the Lord. And everyone who calls on the name of the Lord will be saved; for on Mount Zion and in Jerusalem there will be deliverance, as the Lord has said, even among the survivors whom the Lord calls. (Joel 2:31-32)*

- *He answered, "The one who sowed the good seed is the Son of Man. The field is the world, and the good seed stands for the people of the kingdom. The weeds are the people of the evil one, and the enemy who sows them is the devil. The harvest is the end of the age, and the harvesters are angels. As the weeds are pulled up and burned in the fire, so it will be at the end of the age. The Son of Man will send out his angels, and they will weed out of his kingdom everything that causes sin and all who do evil. They will throw them into the blazing furnace, where there will be weeping and gnashing of teeth. Then the righteous will shine like the sun in the kingdom of their Father. Whoever has ears, let them hear." (Matthew 13:37-43)*

6. Jesus' return will occur after the greatest time of distress the heavens and earth and heavens have ever seen

- *"For then there will be great distress, unequaled from the beginning of the world until now—and never to be equaled again. If those days had not been cut short, no one would survive, but for the sake of the elect those days will be shortened." (Matthew 24:21-22)*

- *See, the Lord is going to lay waste the earth and devastate it; he will ruin its face and scatter its inhabitants—it will be the same for priest as for people, for the master as for his servant, for the mistress as for her servant, for seller as for buyer, for borrower as for lender, for debtor as for creditor. The earth will be completely laid waste and totally plundered. The Lord has spoken this word. The earth dries up and withers, the world languishes and withers, the heavens languish with the earth. The earth is defiled by its people; they have disobeyed the laws, violated the statutes and broken the everlasting covenant. Therefore a curse consumes the earth; its people must bear their guilt. Therefore earth's inhabitants are burned up, and very few are left..." (Isaiah 24:1-6)*

7. Jesus' return will occur at the sound of the final trumpet!

- *"Then will appear the sign of the Son of Man in heaven. And then all the peoples of the earth will mourn when they see the Son of Man coming on the clouds of heaven, with power and great glory. And he will send his angels with a loud trumpet call, and they will gather his elect from the four winds, from one end of the heavens to the other." (Matthew 24:30-31)*

- *For the Lord himself will come down from heaven, with a loud command, with the voice of the archangel and with the trumpet call of God... (I Thessalonians 4:16)*

Some Things the Scriptures Seem Very Clear About

1.   Jesus' return will occur three and one-half years (1,260 days) after the abomination that causes desolation is set up in the temple

- *"So when you see standing in the holy place 'the abomination that causes desolation,' spoken of through the prophet Daniel—let the reader understand—then let those who are in Judea flee to the mountains." (Matthew 24:15-16)*

- *He will confirm a covenant with many for one 'seven.' In the middle of the 'seven' he will put an end to sacrifice and offering. And at the temple he will set up an abomination that causes desolation, until the end that is decreed is poured out on him. (Daniel 9:27)*

- *They will trample on the holy city for 42 months. And I will appoint my two witnesses, and they will prophesy for 1,260 days, clothed in sackcloth. (Revelation 11:2-3)*

- *"It will be for a time, times and half a time. When the power of the holy people has been finally broken, all these things will be completed." (Daniel 12:7)*

2.   The abomination that causes desolation will be set up three and one-half years (1,260 days) after Israel signs the peace treaty with a 10 nation confederation (which includes the beast)

- *He will confirm a covenant with many for one 'seven.' In the middle of the 'seven' he will put an end to sacrifice and offering. And at the temple he will set up an abomination that causes desolation, until the end that is decreed is poured out on him. (Daniel 9:27)*

- *"The ten horns you saw are ten kings who have not yet received a kingdom, but who for one hour will receive authority as kings along with the beast. They have one purpose and will give their power and authority to the beast. They will wage war against the Lamb, but the Lamb will triumph over them because he is Lord of lords and King of kings—and with him will be his called, chosen and faithful followers." (Revelation 17:12-14)*

3.   We will witness the unveiling of seven seal judgments, seven trumpets and seven bowls of wrath during the end times

- The Seven Seals: Revelation 6-8
- The Seven Trumpets: Revelation 8-11
- The Seven Bowls of Wrath: Revelation 15-16

4.   Jesus' return will be announced by the seventh trumpet in Revelation, which is the final trumpet. This is the same trumpet that Jesus mentions in Matthew 24:31. This is also the time of the gathering of the saints to meet Jesus *(also known by the church as the "rapture")*

- There is found only one mention by Jesus of an end time trumpet in all of the Scripture. It is found in Matthew 24:31: *"Immediately after the distress of those days 'the sun will be darkened, and the moon will not give its light; the stars will fall from the sky, and the heavenly bodies will be shaken.' Then will appear the sign of the Son of Man in heaven. And then all the peoples of the earth will mourn when they see the Son of Man coming on the clouds of heaven, with power and great glory. And he will send his angels with a loud trumpet call, and they will gather his elect from the four winds, from one end of the heavens to the other"* (Matthew 24:29-31).

- *For the Lord himself will come down from heaven, with a loud command, with the voice of the archangel and with the trumpet call of God, and the dead in Christ will rise first. After that, we who are still alive and are left will be caught up together with them in the clouds to meet the Lord in the air. And so we will be with the Lord forever. (I Thessalonians 4:16-17)*

- *The Seventh Trumpet*

  The seventh angel sounded his trumpet, and there were loud voices in heaven, which said: "The kingdom of the world has become the kingdom of our Lord and of his Messiah, and he will reign for ever and ever." And the twenty-four elders, who were seated on their thrones before God, fell on their faces and worshiped God, saying: "We give thanks to you, Lord God Almighty, the One who is and who was, because you have taken your great power and have begun to reign. The nations were angry, and your wrath has come." (Revelation 11:15-18)

5. The battle at Armageddon will occur during the time of seven bowls of wrath, which begin after the seventh trumpet

- *I saw in heaven another great and marvelous sign: seven angels with the seven last plagues—last, because with them God's wrath is completed. And I saw what looked like a sea of glass glowing with fire and, standing beside the sea, those who had been victorious over the beast and its image and over the number of its name. They held harps given them by God and sang the song of God's servant Moses and of the Lamb... (Revelation 15:1-3)*

- *The sixth angel poured out his bowl on the great river Euphrates, and its water was dried up to prepare the way for the kings from the East. Then I saw three impure spirits that looked like frogs; they came out of the mouth of the dragon, out of the mouth of the beast and out of the mouth of the false prophet. They are demonic spirits that perform signs, and they go out to the kings of the whole world, to gather them for the battle on the great day of God Almighty. "Look, I come like a thief! Blessed is the one who stays awake and remains clothed, so as not to go naked and be shamefully exposed." Then they gathered the kings together to the place that in Hebrew is called Armageddon. (Revelation 16:12-16)*

6.   Jesus will return, riding on a white horse. Joined by His beloved saints, He will battle and defeat the beast and his armies

- *The Heavenly Warrior Defeats the Beast*

    I saw heaven standing open and there before me was a white horse, whose rider is called Faithful and True. With justice he judges and wages war. His eyes are like blazing fire, and on his head are many crowns. He has a name written on him that no one knows but he himself. He is dressed in a robe dipped in blood, and his name is the Word of God. The armies of heaven were following him, riding on white horses and dressed in fine linen, white and clean. Coming out of his mouth is a sharp sword with which to strike down the nations. "He will rule them with an iron scepter." He treads the winepress of the fury of the wrath of God Almighty. On his robe and on his thigh he has this name written: KING OF KINGS AND LORD OF LORDS (Revelation 19:11-16)

Some Things We Don't Know for Certain from Scripture

1. We don't know the exact timing or location of the birth pangs

- I believe that one reason Jesus commands us to watch and pray is to encourage us to remain in Him. If we knew our final day on this earth, whether by natural causes, accident, catastrophe, major birth pang or seal judgment, we might be tempted to go off and live any way we wish and then attempt to come back to Jesus closer to the time of our demise.

2. We don't know the exact timing of *most* of the seven seals, seven trumpets and seven bowls of wrath

- I believe the exact timing of most of these events are hidden for the same reason that the exact timing of the birth pangs are hidden. However, we are warned of these events repeatedly throughout scripture as well as, for many, through dreams, visions and prophetic words.

- We should expect to see the intensity and frequency of the seals, trumpets and bowls increasing over time. I would personally expect to see them concentrated toward the last three and one-half years at the end of the age.

- I believe we should generally know what is coming next (e.g. the next seal judgment) if we are watching and remaining in the Lord, since we have studied and already know what the seven seals, seven trumpets and seven bowls of wrath consist of.

- I personally expect the bowls of wrath to happen in a rather short period of time, possibly a period of 30 days, beginning after the seventh trumpet has sounded, three and one-half years (1,260 days) after the abomination of desolation is set up.

3.   We don't know all of the details and exact timing of the unfolding of the mysteries of the prophets that will be fulfilled in the days leading up to the seventh trumpet

- *Then the angel I had seen standing on the sea and on the land raised his right hand to heaven. And he swore by him who lives for ever and ever, who created the heavens and all that is in them, the earth and all that is in it, and the sea and all that is in it, and said, "There will be no more delay! But in the days when the seventh angel is about to sound his trumpet, the mystery of God will be accomplished, just as he announced to his servants the prophets." (Revelation 10:5-7)*

4.   When Jesus returns, we don't know how much time He will spend in various places on the earth on His way to fight against His enemies in Jerusalem

- We know that Jesus returns to fight against His enemies that are besieging Jerusalem. However, we find that Isaiah saw Jesus returning through Edom (modern day Jordan). *"God's Day of Vengeance and Redemption: Who is this coming from Edom, from Bozrah, with his garments stained crimson? Who is this, robed in splendor, striding forward in the greatness of his strength? 'It is I, proclaiming victory, mighty to save'"* (Isaiah 63:1).

- *Then the Lord will go out and fight against those nations, as he fights on a day of battle. On that day his feet will stand on the Mount of Olives, east of Jerusalem, and the Mount of Olives will be split in two from east to west, forming a great valley, with half of the mountain moving north and half moving south. You will flee by my mountain valley, for it will extend to Azel. You will flee as you fled from the earthquake in the days of Uzziah king of Judah. Then the Lord my God will come, and all the holy ones with him. (Zechariah 14:3-5)*

- *Judgment on the Whole Earth in the Day of the Lord... ...At that time I will search Jerusalem with lamps and punish those who are complacent, who are like wine left on its dregs, who think, 'The Lord will do nothing, either good or bad.' (Zephaniah 1:1,12)*

- I do find it quite interesting that Jesus makes the following statement during the time when the nations are battling against Jerusalem (which occurs during the sixth bowl of wrath): *"Look, I come like a thief! Blessed is the one who stays awake and remains clothed, so as not to go naked and be shamefully exposed"* (see Revelation 16:15). I mention this because His return should have been evident in the days leading up to the seventh trumpet, or at least upon the sounding of the seventh trumpet. So, I believe this statement could point to a couple of different possibilities:

  i.   When Jesus returns, He may have some time appointed to accomplish tasks at various places across the earth before He fights against His enemies at Jerusalem. As we previously discussed, it seems apparent that the seventh trumpet is 1,260 days after the abomination that causes desolation is set up. Could it be that the bowls of wrath, which culminate in Jesus' battle at Jerusalem, occur during a 30 day period of time? *"From the time that the daily sacrifice is abolished and the abomination that causes desolation is set up, there will be 1,290 days"* (Daniel 12:11). Here is where find an extra 30 days.

ii. Secondly, I believe that Revelation 16:15 highlights the truth that Jesus will come like a thief, not to those who are watching, but to those who are *not* watching.

   - *"Look, I come like a thief! Blessed is the one who stays awake and remains clothed, so as not to go naked and be shamefully exposed."* (Revelation 16:15)

   - *"But understand this: If the owner of the house had known at what time of night the thief was coming, he would have kept watch and would not have let his house be broken into." (Matthew 24:43)*

   - *But if you do not wake up, I will come like a thief, and you will not know at what time I will come to you. (Revelation 3:3)*

   - *But you, brothers and sisters, are not in darkness so that this day should surprise you like a thief. (I Thessalonians 5:4)*

- Lastly, what are Jesus and His followers doing during these extra, and apparently final, 45 days? It is a mystery! And I am certain it is something wonderful and glorious indeed! I imagine it may be the beginning of the new government *(12:12)*, with the King reigning over His Kingdom of Love! *"Blessed is the one who waits for and reaches the end of the 1,335 days"* (Daniel 12:12). *Remember, there is going to be a wedding!*

Signs of the Times and Personal Observations

Jesus admonished us to watch and pray, observing and discerning the signs of the times. That is the responsibility of each one of us. So, I am not afraid to put down a few of my own personal observations and thoughts. I would obviously not desire for you to just adopt my thoughts. I would encourage you to study the Bible, seek, watch, pray and listen to the Holy Spirit, recording your own thoughts.

I think there is one thing that we can know for certain: what we know now about the details of the end times is small compared to what we will know several years from now. The river continues to grow deeper as we approach the end of the age (see Ezekiel 47). The same can be said about prophecy, healings, miracles and other signs and wonders. These things will grow greater as we get closer to the end. This doesn't mean we should be shying away from operating in the small things we have now. We know that if we are responsible with the small things, we will be entrusted with greater things (see Matthew 25:21). So we should engage and operate in what we have today, primarily in love!

So, what I share with you today about when I believe some of these things may happen may seem relatively uninformed a few years from now. However, when a doctor knows that a baby is coming, he is not afraid to give his best estimated due date. As we know, if the baby comes early, it comes early; and if it comes late, it comes late. We know more about the precise timing when we get closer to the baby's birth. It will be the same for the birth of the Kingdom of God on the earth. Let us, therefore, act wisely on what we know today. In the meantime, let us continue to watch and pray, expecting to know more details in the days to come—in His perfect timing.

Signs of the Times

The many signs of the times should alert us to the fact that we are approaching the end of the age. These signs are provided by the great mercy of God for our benefit.

1.   Israel has become a nation again (1948) and Jerusalem returned back to the nation of Israel (1967). Millions of Jewish people have been returning to their homeland. These are among the greatest prophetic signs of the end times (see Genesis 13:14-15; 17:7-8 & Isaiah 11).

2.   The nations are once again beginning to surround Israel to wage war against her. Israel's allies are dwindling (see Luke 21:20, Psalm 83, Zechariah 12:3; 14:1-5 & Joel 31-16).

3.   Anti-Semitism is on the rise once again; we've seen a very large increase over the last few years, especially across Europe. I believe as Israel defends herself in battle, anti-Semitism will dramatically increase across the earth, as will international pressure upon Israel for her to sign a peace deal (see Daniel 9:27 & Revelation 17:12-14).

4.   We've seen unprecedented exponential growth in the number of houses of prayer established with a goal of crying out to the Lord in day and night. Many have estimated 10,000 or more houses of prayer have been established for this purpose in the 21st century alone (see Isaiah 62:1-7 & Luke 18:7-8).

5.   Many largest evangelistic ministries and Bible translators have adopted goals of completing their task of taking the gospel to every tribe, tongue and people by 2025. Some of these ministries are even targeting a completion of 2020. It seems that these goals have been holding more firmly than in the past (see Matthew 13; 24:14 & Revelation 14:14-16).

6.   Many of the largest evangelistic ministries have reported a great increase in the number new followers of Jesus Christ around the world, especially within the 21st century, and even more so within the last few years. One large global ministry that I am familiar with reported more decisions for Christ in the last 10 years than in their previous 55 years of operation. Yet, even within the last few of those 10 years, the number of decisions had grown dramatically! I have recently witnessed many other ministries reporting similar types of growth. All of this points to the beginning and the increase of a great and final harvest (see Matthew 13; 24:14 & Revelation 14:14-16).

7.   The number of movements to Christ among Islam (arguably the 2nd largest religion in the world and historically one of the most difficult to evangelize) has increased exponentially in the 21st century as compared to the 19th and 20th centuries (see Matthew 13; 24:14 & Revelation 14:14-16).

8.   Although sometimes difficult to track in fullness, many ministry sources report that persecution has been exponentially increasing within the 21st century, especially the last few years. For example, Voice of the Martyrs (www.persecution.com), a top ministry to the persecuted church, recently publicly reported twice as many martyrs in 2013 as compared to 2012. I believe we are already seeing a dramatic increase in persecution and martyrdom across the world in 2014 as compared to 2013 (see Matthew 24:9-14, Luke 21:12-19, Revelation 6:9-11 & 7:9-17).

9.   Sin and lawlessness (as well as governmental legislation, endorsement and sponsorship of sin) are increasing. Jesus warns us that the end times will be as the days of Noah and of Lot. In fact, I have been receiving reports from friends in foreign countries describing how the US Government is attempting to pressure the leaders of their governments to legalize, endorse and subsidize sinful activities such as homosexual partnerships and abortion (see Luke 17:26-28, Matthew 24:37-39 & Psalm 94).

10. Signs in the earth, oceans, moon and stars are increasing. I do not think that they are dramatically increasing yet in all types (or categories), but I do think we have seen substantial increases in many categories. I will give a few examples of what I believe are powerful signs. In 2013 we saw the largest tropical cyclone in recorded history ever to reach landfall, and by far the most deadly typhoon ever recorded, resulting in over 10,000 fatalities (Typhoon Haiyan). In 2013 we also saw some of the highest wind speeds in a tornado in recorded history in El Reno, Oklahoma. In 2004 we saw the deadliest tsunami (and deadliest natural disaster) in recorded history, with well over 200,000 fatalities. We have recently seen many extreme

weather records broken. Finally, just this year, we have seen the weakest solar maximum cycle in 100 years. These are all signs that we should be paying attention to; they appear to be indicating an increase in the frequency and intensity of the birth pangs (see Matthew 24:7 & Luke 21:11).

A Few Personal Observations about the Times We Are Now Entering Into

Below are a few of my own person thoughts and observations about the times that we now entering. I hope and pray that you are making some of your own observations and are discussing them with your family and friends.

1.   I personally look at the signs of the times and feel there is a fairly high probability that we will see Jesus Christ return to the earth within the next 7-25 years. I believe that we will know more in the years to come as the signs intensify.

2.   A year or two ago I had an interesting experience. I was reading the Scriptures one day and I felt the Lord telling me to "pay attention to the Jubilees." I hadn't really explored them before. I did some research and found that we are in the 70th Jubilee from the time the Israelites entered the promised land. There is some debate as to when the 70th Jubilee actual ends (many estimates range from 2015 -2030). One could also debate what the significance is, since there isn't anything clearly stated in the Bible about the timing of the 70th Jubilee being related to the end times. However, one thing we do know: at the time of the Jubilee the people of God received back any land that they had sold to foreigners. Could it be that our Lord will get His land back at the end of the 70th Jubilee? (see Joel 2:18). I also find it interesting that

70 Jubilees, which is 70 periods of 7 x 7 years (+ 1 year of celebration), is equal to 7 periods of 70 x 7 (forgiveness and grace). This is also 7 periods of the amount of time that the angel Gabriel told Daniel would transpire before Jesus would first come to the earth. It is just my personal viewpoint that the strongest possible end date for the 70th Jubilee that I've seen is 2024 (the 50th year would be 2025). So, I personally believe that this could be a significant possibility for the return of Jesus. And if this is the year that the Lord returns and gets His land back, then it would follow that we should see a peace deal happen between Israel and a confederation of 10 countries (including the beast) in the 2017-2018 timeframe.

3.   I believe that the escalation of wars between Israel and her neighbors in the next couple of years, especially escalating in 2015, will result in greatly increased pressure on Israel to sign such a peace deal in the near future. But we don't know how long things will go on before this peace deal happens. It could be next year, it could be in a few years, or it could be delayed a decade or two.

4.   There are a few significant historical events that point to the possibility that a peace deal could be signed in 2017. For example, 2017 is 70 years (one of the Biblical definitions of a generation) from the birth of Israel and 50 years (one Jubilee) from when Jerusalem was retaken. Again, I say this to encourage us to watch and pray always. This is not a suggestion to hold on to a specific date.

5.   A few years from now we will know much more, and all of this discussion on timing might seem relatively ignorant. However, I think we have witnessed enough signs already to indicate that we are experiencing exponential acceleration. I

have done quite a bit of forecasting in my career. One thing I've observed is that when things stop growing in a linear fashion and switch to exponential growth, the growth is harder to forecast. I personally believe that the exponential growth in many of these signs make the timing of future events more difficult to predict. So, although it may seem that many things still need to take place before Jesus returns, the exponential rate at which things are happening now make it hard to predict when they will be completed and when the end of the age will reach its fullness.

6.   Personally, I encourage you set your heart to be a sold-out overcomer for Jesus for at least the next 10 years. And always watch and pray! A few years from now we should be able to see if the speed of these signs continues to accelerate. If so, we might see the end of the age unfold even a little sooner than expected. On the other hand, we should soon know if more time will be needed before these things will come to pass. As we continue to watch and pray, we can adjust our relative expectations in regards to timeframes.

7.   If we watch, pray and remain in Him, the Holy Spirit will always let us know what we need to know and say, and at the right time! Therefore, let always stay vigilant and never fall asleep! We should expect in our hearts to increase in the things of God right now *and never stop increasing*. Let us expect to increase in love, increase in unity, increase in prayer, increase in praise, increase in worship, increase in the seeking the presence of the Lord, increase in healing, increase in restoration, increase in the oil of joy, increase in blessing, increase in harvest and increase in the greater works—all to establish the Kingdom of our Bridegroom and King, Jesus Christ, and to destroy the works of Satan on the earth!

16 | HOW WILL WE RESPOND?

Jesus admonished us to watch and pray, observing and discerning the signs of the times. It is clear that this is the responsibility of each one of us. We should not be ignoring the signs, waiting around to see what happens, or trying to figure it all out in our natural minds. We should remain in the love and joy of our Lord Jesus Christ. So, let us keep our ears on the heartbeat of the Father, listening to what the Spirit is saying to us and responding to Him every hour of every day!

Remember that perfect love casts out fear. We are fearless warriors for Christ. So, when we see these signs and wonders begin to take place, we shouldn't fear! He warned us about all of this ahead of time. Patiently endure. Stand firm. Stay sober. Pray always. Love one another. Continue to meet together with the saints, always encouraging one another.

Furthermore, since we know that the time is short, let us join together in love and unity, pressing on to our Bridegroom, King and Judge, Jesus Christ. Let us work together as one and joyfully throw everything we have into the harvest! Let us continue to lead people to Christ, instructing them in righteousness. Let us speak forth the

Kingdom of God until He comes. Always remember, *"When these things begin to take place, stand up and lift up your heads, because your redemption is drawing near."* (Luke 21:28).

Let the Holy Spirit bring you encouragement with these final scriptures.

For, "In just a little while, he who is coming will come and will not delay." And, "But my righteous one will live by faith. And I take no pleasure in the one who shrinks back." (Hebrews 10:37-38)

"Then you will be handed over to be persecuted and put to death, and you will be hated by all nations because of me. At that time many will turn away from the faith and will betray and hate each other, and many false prophets will appear and deceive many people. Because of the increase of wickedness, the love of most will grow cold, but the one who stands firm to the end will be saved. And this gospel of the kingdom will be preached in the whole world as a testimony to all nations, and then the end will come." (Matthew 24:9-14)

Those who are wise will shine like the brightness of the heavens, and those who lead many to righteousness, like the stars for ever and ever. (Daniel 12:3)

Let us hold unswervingly to the hope we profess, for he who promised is faithful. (Hebrews 10:23)

The Spirit and the bride say, "Come!" And let the one who hears say, "Come!" Let the one who is thirsty come; and let the one who wishes take the free gift of the water of life. (Revelation 22:17)

APPENDIX A | A READING LIST

I felt like I couldn't begin writing this book until I had been through the Biblical end times passages at least eight to ten times. So, in about a 2 year period leading up to the writing of this book, I began reading though the following scriptures repeatedly, asking the Holy Spirit to help, and taking down notes as revelation came to me. Not all of the scriptures I studied are only about the end of the age, but most of them are primarily concerning the end times. Other scriptures on this list I simply read to help provide a foundation that would help shed light on the Father's heart concerning His end time plan.

Pentateuch: The First Five Book of the Old Testament

Genesis
Leviticus 26
Numbers 23-24
Deuteronomy 28-30
Deuteronomy 32

Psalms

Psalm 2
Psalm 14
Psalm 24
Psalm 45-50
Psalm 53
Psalm 58-59
Psalm 67-68
Psalm 72
Psalm 75
Psalm 79-80
Psalm 83
Psalm 85
Psalm 87
Psalm 93
Psalm 96-98

Psalm 102
Psalm 110
Psalm 118
Psalm 147
Psalm 149

Old Testament Major Prophets

Isaiah 2
Isaiah 4-5
Isaiah 9
Isaiah 11-14
Isaiah 18-19
Isaiah 21
Isaiah 24-35
Isaiah 40-44
Isaiah 47-53
Isaiah 56
Isaiah 59-66
Jeremiah 30-33
Jeremiah 50-51
Ezekiel 5
Ezekiel 11
Ezekiel 20
Ezekiel 34
Ezekiel 36-39
Ezekiel 40-48
Daniel 2
Daniel 7-9
Daniel 11-12

Old Testament Minor Prophets

Hosea 1-3
Hosea 5-6
Hosea 14
Joel 2-3
Amos 8-9

Obadiah 1
Micah 2
Micah 4-5
Micah 7
Nahum 1
Habakkuk 2-3
Zephaniah 1-3
Zechariah 1-6
Zechariah 8-10
Zechariah 12-14
Malachi 3-4

New Testament

Matthew 8:11-12
Matthew 13
Mathew 24-25
Mark 13
Luke 17-18
Luke 21
I Corinthians 15
II Corinthians 5
I Thessalonians 4-5
II Thessalonians 1-2
II Timothy 3-4
II Peter 3
Revelation

APPENDIX B | THE END TIMES ACCORDING TO JESUS

Many of us have been exposed to widely varied views of the end times by many different theologians, authors, speakers and various forms of media. Have you ever found it all confusing? Have you ever just read what the Bible says about it? Or more specifically, have you ever just read what Jesus has to say about it? One thing I like about Jesus is that He made a couple of strong statements about His end times account: 1) *"See, I have told you ahead of time"* (Matthew 24:25) and 2) *"Heaven and earth will pass away, but my words will never pass away"* (Matthew 24:35). From that, I get the feeling, *"You want the truth? Can you handle the truth? Mark my words, this is how it's going down!"* But how many of us will actually listen? *"Whoever has ears, let them hear."* So, I say in faith, *"But blessed are your eyes because they see, and your ears because they hear"* (Matthew 13:16).

Personally, I have found Jesus' teaching on the end times to be foundational. If I seek to build my understanding of the end times on the "Rock," I know I will be left standing at the end. Once I gain revelation of Jesus' end times teachings, then the end times information in Genesis, Revelation, the Psalms, the Prophets and the Epistles will all begin to be understood with increasing clarity and precision.

Below, I have taken Jesus' end times accounts from Matthew 13, 24 & 25; Mark 13 and Luke 17 & 21. I have combined them together into one long passage. There is quite a bit of overlap between Matthew 24, Mark 13, Luke 17 and Luke 21, so I defaulted to Matthew 24 (the longest account) and only used Mark or Luke where there was a more descriptive version of the verse, or if there was additional information (such as additional verses of scripture). I kept it all in the same chronological order as it appears in the Bible.

A few notes:

- For this study, I used the NIV. There are just a few places where I added in *[brackets]* alternative meanings based on the Greek word used. You may find it interesting to also read these scriptures in other translations.

- I added one personal note and scriptural reference to the NIV's use of "vulture" in Luke 17:37.

- Paul refers to the "trumpet" or "last trumpet" that will sound to call the believers at the end times. Jesus mentions this trumpet only one time in only one of the gospels. See if you can find it (note where and when it occurs).

The End Times According to Jesus

Matthew 13:10-52

10 The disciples came to him and asked, "Why do you speak to the people in parables?"

11 He replied, "Because the knowledge of the secrets of the kingdom of heaven has been given to you, but not to them. 12 Whoever has will be given more, and they will have an abundance. Whoever does not have, even what they have will be taken from them. 13 This is why I speak to them in parables:

"Though seeing, they do not see;

   though hearing, they do not hear or understand.

14 In them is fulfilled the prophecy of Isaiah:

"'You will be ever hearing but never understanding;

   you will be ever seeing but never perceiving.

15 For this people's heart has become calloused;

they hardly hear with their ears,
and they have closed their eyes.
Otherwise they might see with their eyes,
hear with their ears,
understand with their hearts
and turn, and I would heal them.'

16 But blessed are your eyes because they see, and your ears because they hear. 17 For truly I tell you, many prophets and righteous people longed to see what you see but did not see it, and to hear what you hear but did not hear it.

18 "Listen then to what the parable of the sower means: 19 When anyone hears the message about the kingdom and does not understand it, the evil one comes and snatches away what was sown in their heart. This is the seed sown along the path. 20 The seed falling on rocky ground refers to someone who hears the word and at once receives it with joy. 21 But since they have no root, they last only a short time. When trouble or persecution comes because of the word, they quickly fall away. 22 The seed falling among the thorns refers to someone who hears the word, but the worries of this life and the deceitfulness of wealth choke the word, making it unfruitful. 23 But the seed falling on good soil refers to someone who hears the word and understands it. This is the one who produces a crop, yielding a hundred, sixty or thirty times what was sown."

The Parable of the Weeds

24 Jesus told them another parable: "The kingdom of heaven is like a man who sowed good seed in his field. 25 But while everyone was sleeping, his enemy came and sowed weeds among the wheat, and went away. 26 When the wheat sprouted and formed heads, then the weeds also appeared.

27 "The owner's servants came to him and said, 'Sir, didn't

you sow good seed in your field? Where then did the weeds come from?'

28 "'An enemy did this,' he replied.

"The servants asked him, 'Do you want us to go and pull them up?'

29 "'No,' he answered, 'because while you are pulling the weeds, you may uproot the wheat with them. 30 Let both grow together until the harvest. At that time I will tell the harvesters: First collect the weeds and tie them in bundles to be burned; then gather the wheat and bring it into my barn.'"

The Parables of the Mustard Seed and the Yeast

31 He told them another parable: "The kingdom of heaven is like a mustard seed, which a man took and planted in his field. 32 Though it is the smallest of all seeds, yet when it grows, it is the largest of garden plants and becomes a tree, so that the birds come and perch in its branches."

33 He told them still another parable: "The kingdom of heaven is like yeast that a woman took and mixed into about sixty pounds of flour until it worked all through the dough."

34 Jesus spoke all these things to the crowd in parables; he did not say anything to them without using a parable. 35 So was fulfilled what was spoken through the prophet:

"I will open my mouth in parables,

I will utter things hidden since the creation of the world."

The Parable of the Weeds Explained

36 Then he left the crowd and went into the house. His disciples came to him and said, "Explain to us the parable of the weeds in the field."

37 He answered, "The one who sowed the good seed is the Son of Man. 38 The field is the world, and the good seed

stands for the people of the kingdom. The weeds are the people of the evil one, 39 and the enemy who sows them is the devil. The harvest is the end of the age, and the harvesters are angels.

40 "As the weeds are pulled up and burned in the fire, so it will be at the end of the age. 41 The Son of Man will send out his angels, and they will weed out of his kingdom everything that causes sin and all who do evil. 42 They will throw them into the blazing furnace, where there will be weeping and gnashing of teeth. 43 Then the righteous will shine like the sun in the kingdom of their Father. Whoever has ears, let them hear.

The Parables of the Hidden Treasure and the Pearl

44 "The kingdom of heaven is like treasure hidden in a field. When a man found it, he hid it again, and then in his joy went and sold all he had and bought that field.

45 "Again, the kingdom of heaven is like a merchant looking for fine pearls. 46 When he found one of great value, he went away and sold everything he had and bought it.

The Parable of the Net

47 "Once again, the kingdom of heaven is like a net that was let down into the lake and caught all kinds of fish. 48 When it was full, the fishermen pulled it up on the shore. Then they sat down and collected the good fish in baskets, but threw the bad away. 49 This is how it will be at the end of the age. The angels will come and separate the wicked from the righteous 50 and throw them into the blazing furnace, where there will be weeping and gnashing of teeth.

51 "Have you understood all these things?" Jesus asked.

"Yes," they replied.

52 He said to them, "Therefore every teacher of the law

who has become a disciple in the kingdom of heaven is like the owner of a house who brings out of his storeroom new treasures as well as old."

Matthew 24:3-7a

3 As Jesus was sitting on the Mount of Olives, the disciples came to him privately. "Tell us," they said, "when will this happen, and what will be the sign of your coming and of the end of the age?"

4 Jesus answered: "Watch out that no one deceives you. 5 For many will come in my name, claiming, 'I am the Messiah,' and will deceive many. 6 You will hear of wars and rumors of wars, but see to it that you are not alarmed. Such things must happen, but the end is still to come. 7 Nation will rise against nation, and kingdom against kingdom.

Luke 21:11

11 There will be great earthquakes, famines and pestilences in various places, and fearful events and great signs from heaven.

Matthew 24:8

8 All these are the beginning of birth pains.

Mark 13:9,11

9 You must be on your guard. You will be handed over to the local councils and flogged in the synagogues. On account of me you will stand before governors and kings as witnesses to them. 11 Whenever you are arrested and brought to trial, do not worry beforehand about what to say. Just say whatever is given you at the time, for it is not you speaking, but the Holy Spirit.

Luke 21:15

15 For I will give you words and wisdom that none of your adversaries will be able to resist or contradict

Matthew 24:9a

9 "Then you will be handed over to be persecuted and put to death.

Mark 13:12

12 Brother will betray brother to death, and a father his child. Children will rebel against their parents and have them put to death.

Matthew 24:9b-13

...and you will be hated by all nations because of me. 10 At that time many will turn away from the faith and will betray and hate each other, 11 and many false prophets will appear and deceive many people. 12 Because of the increase of wickedness, the love of most will grow cold,

13 but the one who stands firm to the end will be saved.

Luke 21:18-19

18 But not a hair of your head will perish. 19 Stand firm, and you will win life.

Matthew 24:14

14 And this gospel of the kingdom will be preached in the whole world as a testimony to all nations, and then the end will come.

Luke 21:20

20 "When you see Jerusalem being surrounded by armies, you will know that its desolation is near.

Matthew 24:15-16

15 "...when you see standing in the holy place 'the abomination that causes desolation, spoken of through the prophet Daniel—let the reader understand— 16 then let those who are in Judea flee to the mountains.

Luke 21:21b-22

21b ...let those in the city get out, and let those in the country not enter the city. 22 For this is the time of punishment in fulfillment of all that has been written.

Matthew 24:17-21

17 Let no one on the housetop go down to take anything out of the house. 18 Let no one in the field go back to get their cloak. 19 How dreadful it will be in those days for pregnant women and nursing mothers! 20 Pray that your flight will not take place in winter or on the Sabbath. 21 For then there will be great distress, unequaled from the beginning of the world until now—and never to be equaled again.

Luke 21:23b-24

23b There will be great distress in the land and wrath against this people. 24 They will fall by the sword and will be taken as prisoners to all the nations. Jerusalem will be trampled on by the Gentiles until the times of the Gentiles are fulfilled.

Matthew 24:22-26

22 "If those days had not been cut short, no one would survive, but for the sake of the elect those days will be shortened. 23 At that time if anyone says to you, 'Look, here is the Messiah!' or, 'There he is!' do not believe it. 24 For false messiahs and false prophets will appear and perform great signs and wonders to deceive, if possible, even the elect.

25 See, I have told you ahead of time.

26 "So if anyone tells you, 'There he is, out in the wilderness,' do not go out; or, 'Here he is, in the inner rooms,' do not believe it.

Luke 17:23b-24

23b Do not go running off after them. 24 For the Son of Man in his day will be like the lightning, which flashes and lights up the sky from one end to the other

Matthew 24:29

29 "Immediately after the distress of those days
"'the sun will be darkened,
    and the moon will not give its light;
the stars will fall from the sky,
    and the heavenly bodies will be shaken.'

Luke 17:215b-26

25b On the earth, nations will be in anguish and perplexity at the roaring and tossing of the sea. 26 People will faint from terror, apprehensive of what is coming on the world, for the heavenly bodies will be shaken.

Matthew 24:30-31

30 "Then *[or at that time]* will appear the sign of the Son of Man in heaven. And then all the peoples of the earth will mourn when they see the Son of Man coming on the clouds of heaven, with power and great glory. 31 And he will send his angels with a loud trumpet call, and they will gather his elect from the four winds...

Mark 13:27b

...from the ends of the earth to the ends of the heavens.

Luke 21:28

28 When these things begin to take place, stand up and lift up your heads, because your redemption is drawing near."

Matthew 24:32-39a

32 "Now learn this lesson from the fig tree: As soon as its twigs get tender and its leaves come out, you know that summer is near. 33 Even so, when you see all these things, you know that it is near, right at the door. 34 Truly I tell you, this generation will certainly not pass away until all these things have happened. 35 Heaven and earth will pass away, but my words will never pass away.

The Day and Hour Unknown

36 "But about that day or hour no one knows, not even the angels in heaven, nor the Son, but only the Father. 37 As it was in the days of Noah, so it will be at the coming of the Son of Man. 38 For in the days before the flood, people were eating and drinking, marrying and giving in marriage, up to the day Noah entered the ark; 39 and they knew nothing

about what would happen until the flood came and took them all away.

Luke 17:28-37

28 "It was the same in the days of Lot. People were eating and drinking, buying and selling, planting and building. 29 But the day Lot left Sodom, fire and sulfur rained down from heaven and destroyed them all.

30 "It will be just like this on the day the Son of Man is revealed. 31 On that day no one who is on the housetop, with possessions inside, should go down to get them. Likewise, no one in the field should go back for anything. 32 Remember Lot's wife! 33 Whoever tries to keep their life will lose it, and whoever loses their life will preserve it. 34 I tell you, on that night two people will be in one bed; one will be taken and the other left. 35 Two women will be grinding grain together; one will be taken and the other left." [36]

37 "Where, Lord?" they asked.

He replied, "Where there is a dead body, there the vultures *[or "eagles" (i.e. scavenger birds)]*[1] will gather."

Luke 21:34-36

34 "Be careful, or your hearts will be weighed down with carousing, drunkenness and the anxieties of life, and that day will close on you suddenly like a trap. 35 For it will come on all those who live on the face of the whole earth. 36 Be always on the watch, and pray that you may be able *[or "be strengthened"]*[2] to escape *[or "run away" or "flee from"]*[3] all that is about to happen, and that you may be able to stand before the Son of Man."

Matthew 24:42-44

42 "Therefore keep watch, because you do not know on what day your Lord will come. 43 But understand this: If the owner of the house had known at what time of night the thief was coming, he would have kept watch and would not have let his house be broken into. 44 So you also must be ready, because the Son of Man will come at an hour when you do not expect him.

Mark 13:36

36 If he comes suddenly, do not let him find you sleeping. 37 What I say to you, I say to everyone: 'Watch!'"

Matthew 24:45-51

45 "Who then is the faithful and wise servant, whom the master has put in charge of the servants in his household to give them their food at the proper time? 46 It will be good for that servant whose master finds him doing so when he returns. 47 Truly I tell you, he will put him in charge of all his possessions. 48 But suppose that servant is wicked and says to himself, 'My master is staying away a long time,' 49 and he then begins to beat his fellow servants and to eat and drink with drunkards. 50 The master of that servant will come on a day when he does not expect him and at an hour he is not aware of. 51 He will cut him to pieces and assign him a place with the hypocrites, where there will be weeping and gnashing of teeth.

Matthew 25:1-46

"At that time the kingdom of heaven will be like ten virgins who took their lamps and went out to meet the bridegroom. 2 Five of them were foolish and five were wise.

3 The foolish ones took their lamps but did not take any oil with them. 4 The wise ones, however, took oil in jars along with their lamps. 5 The bridegroom was a long time in coming, and they all became drowsy and fell asleep.

6 "At midnight the cry rang out: 'Here's the bridegroom! Come out to meet him!'

7 "Then all the virgins woke up and trimmed their lamps. 8 The foolish ones said to the wise, 'Give us some of your oil; our lamps are going out.'

9 "'No,' they replied, 'there may not be enough for both us and you. Instead, go to those who sell oil and buy some for yourselves.'

10 "But while they were on their way to buy the oil, the bridegroom arrived. The virgins who were ready went in with him to the wedding banquet. And the door was shut.

11 "Later the others also came. 'Lord, Lord,' they said, 'open the door for us!'

12 "But he replied, 'Truly I tell you, I don't know you.'

13 "Therefore keep watch, because you do not know the day or the hour.

The Parable of the Bags of Gold

14 "Again, it will be like a man going on a journey, who called his servants and entrusted his wealth to them. 15 To one he gave five bags of gold, to another two bags, and to another one bag, each according to his ability. Then he went on his journey. 16 The man who had received five bags of gold went at once and put his money to work and gained five bags more. 17 So also, the one with two bags of gold gained two more. 18 But the man who had received one bag went off, dug a hole in the ground and hid his master's money.

19 "After a long time the master of those servants returned and settled accounts with them. 20 The man who

had received five bags of gold brought the other five. 'Master,' he said, 'you entrusted me with five bags of gold. See, I have gained five more.'

21 "His master replied, 'Well done, good and faithful servant! You have been faithful with a few things; I will put you in charge of many things. Come and share your master's happiness!'

22 "The man with two bags of gold also came. 'Master,' he said, 'you entrusted me with two bags of gold; see, I have gained two more.'

23 "His master replied, 'Well done, good and faithful servant! You have been faithful with a few things; I will put you in charge of many things. Come and share your master's happiness!'

24 "Then the man who had received one bag of gold came. 'Master,' he said, 'I knew that you are a hard man, harvesting where you have not sown and gathering where you have not scattered seed. 25 So I was afraid and went out and hid your gold in the ground. See, here is what belongs to you.'

26 "His master replied, 'You wicked, lazy servant! So you knew that I harvest where I have not sown and gather where I have not scattered seed? 27 Well then, you should have put my money on deposit with the bankers, so that when I returned I would have received it back with interest.

28 "'So take the bag of gold from him and give it to the one who has ten bags. 29 For whoever has will be given more, and they will have an abundance. Whoever does not have, even what they have will be taken from them. 30 And throw that worthless servant outside, into the darkness, where there will be weeping and gnashing of teeth.'

The Sheep and the Goats

31 "When the Son of Man comes in his glory, and all the

angels with him, he will sit on his glorious throne. 32 All the nations will be gathered before him, and he will separate the people one from another as a shepherd separates the sheep from the goats. 33 He will put the sheep on his right and the goats on his left.

34 "Then the King will say to those on his right, 'Come, you who are blessed by my Father; take your inheritance, the kingdom prepared for you since the creation of the world. 35 For I was hungry and you gave me something to eat, I was thirsty and you gave me something to drink, I was a stranger and you invited me in, 36 I needed clothes and you clothed me, I was sick and you looked after me, I was in prison and you came to visit me.'

37 "Then the righteous will answer him, 'Lord, when did we see you hungry and feed you, or thirsty and give you something to drink? 38 When did we see you a stranger and invite you in, or needing clothes and clothe you? 39 When did we see you sick or in prison and go to visit you?'

40 "The King will reply, 'Truly I tell you, whatever you did for one of the least of these brothers and sisters of mine, you did for me.'

41 "Then he will say to those on his left, 'Depart from me, you who are cursed, into the eternal fire prepared for the devil and his angels. 42 For I was hungry and you gave me nothing to eat, I was thirsty and you gave me nothing to drink, 43 I was a stranger and you did not invite me in, I needed clothes and you did not clothe me, I was sick and in prison and you did not look after me.'

44 "They also will answer, 'Lord, when did we see you hungry or thirsty or a stranger or needing clothes or sick or in prison, and did not help you?'

45 "He will reply, 'Truly I tell you, whatever you did not do for one of the least of these, you did not do for me.'

46 "Then they will go away to eternal punishment, but the righteous to eternal life."

NOTES:

1. Strong, *Strong's Concordance*, ref. no. 105. Greek word aetos, which means, "an eagle, bird of prey." Whether vulture or eagle, they are both known by their diets to be scavenger birds (although the eagle is both a predator and a scavenger). This understanding is also clarified in Deuteronomy. Note the head of the list of fowl that should not be eaten, *"But these you may not eat: the eagle, the vulture, the black vulture..."* (Deuteronomy 14:12-18)

2. Strong, *Strong's Concordance*, ref. no. 2729. Greek word katischuó, which means, "I prevail against, overpower, get the upper hand."

3. Strong, *Strong's Concordance*, ref. no. 1628. Greek word ekpheugó. which means "I flee out, away, escape; with an acc: I escape something."

ABOUT THE AUTHOR

Stuart and his wife, Heidi, have 40 years of collective experience in various forms of ministry and business. Their areas of focus have been a unique and diverse blend of prayer, mentorship, evangelism, outreach, strategy, marketing, product management, real estate, design and mixed martial arts. Stuart and Heidi reside in Oklahoma, and have seven children.

www.ingramcontent.com/pod-product-compliance
Lightning Source LLC
Chambersburg PA
CBHW031545040426
42452CB00006B/197